A Rogue but Invaluable Book on Financial Planning - Warnings, Proven
Strategies, Myths, and Lagniappe (a little Something Extra)

FINANCIAL PLANNING
REVOLUTIONIZED

Money Doesn't Exist Until You Spend It

It's a wise man who lives with money in the bank;
it's a fool who dies with it. French Proverb

JAMES LAHAM CPA & CONSULTANT

ISBN: 978-1-6847-0710-2 (sc)
ISBN: 978-1-6847-0709-6 (e)

Library of Congress Control Number: 2019908790

Lulu Publishing Services rev. date: 07/09/2019

To my grandson Nicholas—
the happiest and coolest kid ever

ACKNOWLEDGMENTS

I would like to thank my good friend and colleague Jackie Sutton, who patiently translated my handwriting into this typed manuscript—at all times of the day and night.

I also want to thank my good friends and partners in crime CPA Brian Fisher and attorney Mark Malek for their help in keeping me from going off the rails with my content.

Lastly, I want to thank all the wonderful clients, colleagues, and friends I have had the great pleasure of working with over the years. They were the force behind this book.

WHY WRITE THIS BOOK?

I have been a CPA since 1974, specializing in taxation and financial consulting, and I have worked with thousands of companies and clients over the years in their quest for prosperity and financial freedom. Most have been successful, but many have crashed and burned, often because of bad decisions that were within their control.

I liken my experience to the Farmers Insurance commercial that uses the slogan "We know a thing or two because we have seen a thing or two."

That is how I feel. I know a thing or two because I have seen a thing or two. I have seen many financial-planning strategies play out successfully, but I have also seen many failures and calamities. These experiences have been with real people, and most of them have been clients for years. I have seen their ups and downs, and I have witnessed how finances emotionally affect their lives. I will share with you what I have learned from more than forty-five years of practice in the financial world, working with actual clients and hundreds of investment advisers within that time frame.

This is not a how-to book, and it is not intended to change lives, but if the book does help you in any way, that would be most gratifying. What you are about to read will be contrary to some of the financial-planning concepts of many Main Street financial advisers. I am here not to abandon those traditional concepts but to point out that some of them are flawed, at least in part, largely because of the misunderstanding of the human emotional element embedded in all financial affairs.

This book lays out some warnings to consider, some solid financial-planning principles, a variety of financial-planning myths, and, my favorite, lagniappe. Lagniappe is a good old Cajun word that means "a little something extra." I will throw in some fun "little something extra" financial strategies along the way as my lagniappe.

I hope you have some fun with this book as well, and by all means, do not take any of this—or life in general—too seriously. As the Cajuns are quick to say, "Laissez les bons temps rouler" (Let the good times roll), and maybe some of these financial tips will give you a little more money to play with.

WHERE DID THAT CRAZY EXPRESSION "MONEY DOESN'T EXIST UNTIL YOU SPEND IT" COME FROM?

In 1994 I read Tom Clancy's *Debt of Honor* and was fascinated by it. I remember being at my brother Rene's house in Antigo, Wisconsin, during the Christmas holiday when I read it. I got up several mornings at four o'clock, made coffee, built a fire, and read that book until I finished it. It was that good!

The premise of the book is that certain brilliant Japanese zealots wanted to even the score from World War II with multiple forms of attacks on the United States. Sound familiar? The first attack absolutely fascinated me. It was not a military attack; it was an attack on our financial system. The Japanese invested heavily in a group of mutual funds so they could manipulate them by infiltrating their recording and reporting systems. In an incredible cyberattack, they put our financial system in chaos. As I recall, they eventually messed with the accounting and investment reporting for investors so they no longer had access to their accounts. No one could tell them what they actually owned. In a real sense, their wealth just vanished overnight.

Fast-forward to now, some twenty-five years later, where virtually everything is digital, and substitute the Russians or the Chinese for the Japanese. Ponder that scary thought for a minute!

You may be saying to yourself, "That's one hell of a story, but what does it have to do with this Chapter of the book?" Well, let me tell you.

Shortly after reading Clancy's incredible book, we were immersed in tax season. I was meeting with one of my wealthy clients. He had "tons of money," but he was beyond frugal. He was driving an old car, was not charitable, and really was not at all happy or pleasant for a person who had so much.

I was reviewing his investments from a major brokerage house, which showed that he had millions of dollars in stocks and bonds. I said to him, Mr. Crabby, "Do you think you have millions of dollars?"

He finally grinned and said very proudly, "Absolutely!"

I then asked, "How do you know?"

He responded, "Well, it's all right in front of you."

I said, "I don't see millions of dollars anywhere. I just see a piece of paper that says you have millions of dollars. Where are the millions of dollars—and how do you know they are there?"

At that point, he turned ashen and said, "What are you trying to tell me?"

I said, "Well, dumbass"—I didn't really say that, but that's what I meant—"money doesn't exist until you spend it!" I told him he should consider spending some of it wisely and some of it just for fun while he was still healthy and able to do so.

So there you have it. That is where the title of this book comes from. Money is fiction and does not become a reality until it is spent on something. It is also a hell of a lot more fun when you spend it on yourself because somebody is going to spend it someday—and why shouldn't that be you? I can absolutely assure you that when you leave it to your giddy heirs, they will have no problem spending it without hesitation, dumbass.

A SHORT CHAPTER OF SUBSTANCE

Ninety-five percent of economics is common sense made complicated.
—Ha-Joon Chang, South Korean economist

Ninety-five percent of investing is common sense made complicated.
—James S. LaHam, CPA and author

CONTENTS

CHAPTER 1

It Takes a Long, Painful Time to Make Up Lost Ground

The Dow Jones Index fell from a peak of 14,164 on October 9, 2007, to 6,443 on March 6, 2009, registering a 54 percent drop during the Great Recession of 2008. So if you had invested in an index fund that tracked the Dow Jones, your $100,000 at the start of the recession was reduced to $46,000 seventeen months later. You may ask, "Just how long would it take with an 8 percent compounded rate of return to get back your original $100,000 investment?"

Well, read it and weep! It would take ten long, painful years to get back to the beginning.

That means that if you were forty years old at the time the recession started, you got back to your original investment at age fifty. If you were fifty at that time, you got back to your original investment at sixty. And God forbid if you invested $100,000 at age sixty. Then you had to wait until age seventy to get back to your original $100,000. If you factor in that inflation took away about 25 percent of your purchasing power during those ten years, your $100,000 ten-year investment actually was worth only $75,000. This is a painful financial principle you must take to heart as you consider your risk tolerance. Do not take it lightly.

CHAPTER 2

Investment Euphoria Followed by
Investment Panic Is Devastating, Scaring
You into the Right Investment Mind-Set

Most financial advisers recite the overworked statement to "stay the course." But those advisers don't make it painfully clear what that actually means and how much discipline it takes under extreme stress to stay the course. Unfortunately, it has been my experience that few people stay the course when we have a plunging market. Instead, they crack and sell. I don't disagree with staying the course—but only if you have a balanced portfolio, as we discuss throughout this book. The purpose of this chapter is to absolutely frighten you into developing a well-thought-out investment portfolio that is balanced and diverse.

The human emotional reality is that it feels so natural to buy more stock and stay the course when markets are going up. Many investors blindly raise their exposure to stocks that have gotten more expensive and ignore the reality that future returns will almost certainly be less or negative.

Investors are notorious for chasing overperformance by relying on prior performance and ending up with underperformance because they don't heed the footnote in all investment publications: "Prior investment performance cannot be relied on to predict future performance."

History and human behavior have shown that investors and advisers still have an inclination to chase performance and panic a little or a lot during a severe recession or a collapsing market. Extreme volatility triggers emotional responses that will screw up the best-laid investment plan. I have found that the older and wealthier you are, the more likely you are to sell off irrationally. The pain of loss is overwhelming and debilitating compared to the subtle warmth enjoyed with investment gains. The feeling of not being in control and the panic-driven decision to sell always seem better than sitting back and doing nothing as you see your wealth meter drop from week to week.

Let's put this into a simple example to quantify the two extremes of the market. Let's say you have earned a spectacular 100 percent on the $100,000 you put into an equity fund in 2009, so your fund is now worth $200,000. You are so delighted with the ten-year up market that you put in another $100,000 just before global markets begin to fall, based on a series of economic and political events. Your fund loses 50 percent in the aftermath of a bad market, leaving you with $150,000—or a net loss of $50,000.

You say that the math just cannot be correct, so let's piece it together. You put in $100,000 in 2009 and made $100,000 over the next ten years, so you now have $200,000. You now add $100,000 to the fund as reports show a robust economy and pundits say the future is still bright. However, the timing isn't good, as you put in the money just prior to the next recession. You slug through a two-year severe bear market, losing 50 percent of your fund's value, so you now have $150,000 (50 percent x $300,000), losing $50,000 of your original investment principal over the twelve-year period.

I realize this is an extreme example, but it does illustrate several points.

Do not chase prior performance, because it can be terribly misleading. I see this prevalent trend in 401(k) plans, where people look only at prior performance to choose their fund mix.

The economy has always been cyclical, so what goes up will go down. A balanced and diverse portfolio is essential to managing investment volatility and reducing emotional tension.

Don't try to time the market; no one has that divine skill.

You should enter the market on a steady and regular basis, putting similar amounts into your investment plan monthly. This is known as *dollar-cost averaging.* It will avoid the disaster noted above by not putting large amounts in at one time.

It is a long, painful crawl to recover the money you have lost in a down market, especially if you have been foolishly invested by chasing yields that are impossible to sustain over time.

Well, I hope I have scared the living hell out of you and have motivated you to invest using the sensible methods discussed throughout this book. Investing simply requires a solid strategy, discipline, and patience. Good luck—and get started today. Then sit back and relax, knowing you have entered the investment arena under the right conditions.

CHAPTER 3

Start Small—but Don't Think Small, and Don't Forget to Invest in Memories along the Way

I was aware of financial planning at a fairly young age, but it certainly was not my focus. At age thirty, I was at a consulting conference, and there was a session by a husband-and-wife financial advisory team. They were insightful, and the group was mostly people in their early thirties and not in the saving mind-set. The advisers made a simple but powerful point to start saving something now, however modest, to use the power of compounded interest over a long period of time to build your wealth. The simple message was to put 5 to 15 percent of your income into long-term savings, which could include retirement accounts.

That was a much easier message to take than the painful budget approach many advisers recommend. The budget approach is a hopeless, time-consuming process that does not work for most people and creates extreme tension in relationships. That was a great message because everyone can do 5 percent, perhaps 10 percent, and ideally 15 percent, depending on your personal situation, family, housing needs, and other factors.

There is an old savings formula that says you should spend 50 percent on necessities, 30 percent on discretionary spending, and 20 percent on savings. The new wisdom says if you get started between ages twenty-five and thirty, 15 percent will get you there at retirement. Obviously, the more you save, the bigger your treasure chest will be in the future. However, as I discuss later, you must also live in the moment, as that is truly all we are guaranteed! This requires finding a happy medium by balancing your savings and spending habits to enjoy life now while providing for a successful retirement.

Nonetheless, this savings strategy is ridiculously simple and effective. You calculate 15 percent of your pretax income and put that into savings and retirement accounts and then just spend the rest and have fun. The key is to just get started at some level and stick with it, as we all know that getting started is more than half the battle.

The above financial lesson was certainly valuable, but the nontraditional advice that blew me away was the unexpected advice to also "invest in memories" along the way because that is an essential part of a sound financial plan. What a refreshing approach to financial planning that incorporates the current with the future! The point is to responsibly invest in important things in your current life, such as holidays, birthdays, anniversaries, and affordable and meaningful vacations.

We all know how fragile life can be. You must seize the moment, working in your personal celebrations and investing in memories that will indeed be with you forever. Be financially wise, but don't save yourself into the poorhouse. You got that?

CHAPTER 4

Invest for the Long Haul, but Have a Disciplined Plan, as Only Fools Invest without One

---

I have always been fascinated with economist Harry M. Markowitz. The 1990 Nobel laureate in economics is considered the father of modern portfolio theory. He is a genius who wrote his thesis, entitled "Portfolio Selection," in 1952. Go forward almost seventy years, and the basic premise of his portfolio management remains a sound investment theory and process.

The basic concept is that rational investors should assemble a diversified portfolio of stocks and bonds with a mix of risk and return optimized for their own needs and beliefs. The fundamental premise of Markowitz's theory on portfolio management is to invest regularly in low-cost stock and bond index funds instead of individual stocks and bonds. The irrefutable truth is that there is no one on earth who can consistently pick winning stocks or bonds as the markets are very much like sports betting. You may bet correctly on several winning stocks only to be slapped with a big loser that wipes out all of those winners. If you actually think you or your adviser is smarter than this, think again, my friend. Consider that Facebook lost 26 percent, or $130 billion, in two hours of trading on July 25, 2018. That is more than the entire market value of Starbucks and American Express. Enough said! Just remember that the casino always wins in the end. Stick with Mr. Markowitz and don't try to play the market. Have a well-thought-out plan and execute it.

The simplest plan is to buy stock and bond index funds over time and allocate them in a proportion that gives you a level of volatility and security that you are comfortable with. This part is unique to each individual as goals, age, wealth, and security are truly unique to each investor. You then periodically rebalance your investment mix between stock funds and fixed income funds as market values change. For example, say your comfort level is to have 60 percent in stock index funds and 40 percent in fixed income funds (*target allocation*). With the strong run-up in the value of stock funds over recent years, your relative market values now are 75 percent stock funds and 25 percent fixed income funds. To get rebalanced, you would take profits and sell some of your stock funds and reinvest the proceeds into fixed income funds to get back to your target allocation of 60 percent to 40 percent. Nice and neat, disciplined and according to your plan.

Mr. Markowitz often noted that investor behavior is often idiosyncratic, unpredictable, and complex, which in itself creates market uncertainty because of the human element and emotions. Accordingly, a disciplined investment plan following these basic investment fundamentals is likely the best investment policy for most investors.

Mr. Markowitz is approaching ninety-one years old as of this writing, and those who heed his wisdom and advice will become successful investors if they regularly follow the plan and rebalance and reallocate as time and needs change. It is that simple.

Let's now look at how you implement this stay-the-course strategy. The absolute simplest way is to find a *balanced mutual fund*, which by design is a diverse portfolio of let's say 60 percent equities and 40 percent fixed income. These are very simple and effective funds if you stay the course and invest on a regular monthly basis (whatever the amount). This *dollar-cost averaging* disciplined investment pattern takes out market and emotional timing.

Speaking from a real personal experience, Vanguard came out with the STAR Fund in 1985, which was one of the first significant *balanced funds*. My boss at that time, Fred Braun, told me it would be wise to start an IRA and put the maximum amount of $2,000 into this new Vanguard STAR Fund. That fund has done an average of 9.48 percent annual return since inception. I did invest in that fund for many years and had I continued to put in $2,000 each year through 2018, my total investment of $68,000 would be worth $479,175 today. That is the miracle of compounding and simple, disciplined investing.

Let's make this even more interesting and bring this up to date. Let's assume that you put in the maximum amount of $18,500, which adjusts with inflation, into your 401(k) for thirty-four years, which only costs you $13,000 in cash flow each year because of the tax savings. The $629,000 you put in over thirty-four years, which you were only out $440,000 in cash flow, turns into $4,432,371 by just putting in a manageable amount each year without fail. That is an incredible result.

There are several quality balanced fund alternatives in the market. Some of them are actively managed like Vanguard's Wellington, T. Rowe Price Balanced, and Oakmark Equity & Income. You can go with indexed and passively managed funds like the Vanguard Balanced Index Fund. Most of the large fund families, like Vanguard, American Funds, BlackRock, and Fidelity, have various options. Before we leave the simple balanced fund option, it is important to note that in the past ten years, balanced funds averaged almost 6 percent annualized returns, compared to 5.5 percent for the average of total return funds—not bad for simplicity and manageable volatility.

In the next few chapters, we will look at some variations to this investment theme. Trust me—it will get more interesting.

CHAPTER 5

Bogleheads Rock: The Three-Fund Portfolio Approach

In the previous chapter, I suggested that the simplest method of investing for the long haul is the use of a balanced mutual fund, or a variation of this using a *target date fund*. This *one-pot-meal method* of investing cannot get any simpler, and it does achieve diversity and balance. If you are just getting started on your investment journey, this may be the way to go.

In this chapter, we are going to introduce another simple investment strategy that uses a three–mutual fund investment approach. This methodology was brought into the spotlight recently with the June 2018 publication of *The Bogleheads' Guide to the Three-Fund Portfolio*. If you are not familiar with the term "Bogleheads," they are avid followers of the iconic founder of the Vanguard mutual funds, John C. Bogle. Mr. Bogle is certainly one of the pioneers of broad-based investing, and he is one of the most famous and most respected financial strategists of our time. Unfortunately, Mr. Bogle passed away on January 16, 2019, amidst endless accolades from the financial community, and is perhaps the most influential person ever in the stock market.

The Vanguard mutual fund company is unique in that it is owned by its investors and not outside stockholders. This fact has resulted in the expenses of the funds being less than many other mutual fund companies. It is important to note that as I am writing this, Fidelity Funds and other fund companies are at war with each other, reducing some of their fees to 0 percent. This certainly begs the question as to how these funds are making a profit. Stay tuned on this as there may be more to the story—and just be aware.

Regardless of those new developments, Vanguard recently reported "that for the 10-year period ending September 30, 2018, 9 of 9 Vanguard money market funds, 55 of 58 Vanguard bond funds, 22 of 22 Vanguard balanced funds, and 128 of 137 Vanguard stock funds, or 94.7 percent of all of the funds outperformed their Lipper peer-group averages."

There are certainly many other high-quality and low-cost funds available (we will discuss some later), but the Vanguard funds are usually a good choice. Incidentally, I highly recommend the Bogleheads book; at only 112 pages, it is very informative and is an easy and fun nontechnical read.

Now that you have a little background, let's get back to the Bogleheads book on the simplicity and effectiveness of investing in just three total market index funds to achieve attractive yields with relatively high safety and security. I will be the first to admit, along with thousands of others, that this investment strategy is one of my favorites. It is a little spicier and more fun than just going the single *balanced fund* route.

The Boglehead guide recommends the following three funds as your investment vehicles:

- Vanguard Total Stock Market Index Investor Shares (VTSMX) and Admiral Shares (VTSAX). These are the same fund, but Admiral Shares have a lower expense ratio as they require a larger investment (at least $10,000). This fund owns more than 3,500 US company stocks, and expense ratios are 0.15 percent and 0.04 percent, respectively.
- Vanguard Total Bond Market Index Fund Investor Shares (VBMFX) and Admiral Shares (VBTLX). This fund owns more than eight thousand diversified, high-quality US bonds, with respective expense ratios of 0.18 percent and 0.12 percent.
- Vanguard Total International Stock Index Fund Investor Shares (VGTSZ), with respective expense ratios of 0.18 percent and 0.12 percent. This fund invests in more than seventeen thousand diversified, nonoverlapping, worldwide securities.

We have now achieved the first fundamental of investing, which is *diversification*. This mix of funds gets you a broad range of stocks, bonds, and international securities. Combined, they will offer balance, more consistent investment returns, and less volatility.

The second fundamental of investing is known as *asset allocation*, which is simply how you want to allocate your investment dollars between the three funds. This is very important because this part of the investment equation changes with your age and risk tolerance. This strategy requires you to actively monitor your allocations because your relative fund balances change automatically as the market values of your funds change.

One of the simplest and most valuable allocation formulas is to just subtract your current age from one hundred. This difference is what your allocation should be between stocks and bonds. For example, if you are thirty, you would invest 70 percent in stocks and 30 percent in bonds. If you are sixty, you would invest 40 percent in stocks and 60 percent in bonds. This formula supports one of our main goals, which is to have less volatility and more stability as you get closer to retirement. As a slight variation to this classic standard, I believe the formula should change from 100 to 105 to account for longer life expectancies. For example, if you are age thirty, your stock to bond allocation would be 75 percent stock and 25 percent bonds.

I should also point out that it has been my experience that *endowment funds* of nonprofit institutions usually stay in the 60 percent stocks and 40 percent bond range, with some closer to 50 percent each, but they almost never go beyond 65 percent stocks and 35 percent bonds. If you sit on a nonprofit board of directors, you have a legal fiduciary duty to the institution to err on the more conservative side of investing. This revelation gives you another reference point to consider as you choose your own personal allocations. I think it is important to point this out because these institutions naturally are more cautious in their investments, and you may want to follow their lead.

The last thing you need to determine in your investment decision is how much of your stock allocation should go to international equities. Keep in mind that Bloomberg reported that as of March 2017, the US markets controlled only about 36.5 percent of the total worldwide market value. In other words, foreign markets controlled 63.5 percent of the world market value, which means that your investment allocation should have a significant portion in foreign stock markets to achieve balance and stability.

The obvious question at this point is what percentage of your stock allocation should go into foreign stocks. Taylor Larimore, the author of *The Bogleheads' Guide* suggests 20 percent of your stock portion should go into foreign stock markets. He gets to 20 percent based on John Bogle's personal recommendation that a maximum of 20 percent of your stock investments should go into foreign markets. Vanguard's own study suggests that a minimum of 20 percent should go into foreign markets, and it should not exceed 40 percent. This really is a personal choice, which makes this overall strategy a bit more interactive and interesting.

Before we get into some analytics, I should point out that Vanguard is by no means the only fund you can use. You could use, for example, Fidelity's Total Market Index Fund, Fidelity's US Bond Index Fund, and the Fidelity Global ex US Fund as your investment fund group. Schwab offers similar funds as well. All of these are quality funds, and you should go with the family of funds you feel most comfortable with.

In fact, *Money* magazine's February 2019 issue listed their fifty best mutual funds and their fifty best exchange-traded funds (ETFs). Exchange-traded funds trade throughout the day like stocks. In this article, *Money* offered the following three sample portfolios that are variations and alternatives to the Boglehead model. These portfolios illustrate how you can tailor your investing based on your own personal preferences:

Using ETFs to Go Simple

Schwab US Broad Market ETF	30 percent
Vanguard Total international Stock ETF	20 percent
Vanguard REIT ETF	10 percent
Vanguard Total International Bond ETF	10 percent
Vanguard Total Bond Market ETF	30 percent
Total	100 percent

Using ETFs to Tilt Toward Values

Vanguard Total Bond Market ETF	30 percent
Schwab US Broad Market ETF	25 percent
Vanguard Total International Stock ETF	15 percent
Vanguard Total International Bond ETF	10 percent
Vanguard REIT ETF	10 percent
Vanguard Value ETF	5 percent
Vanguard Small-Cap Value ETF	5 percent
Total	100 percent

Using Traditional Funds That Are Actively Managed

Schwab Total Stock Market Index	25 percent
Vanguard Total Bond Market Index	20 percent
Vanguard Total International Stock Index	15 percent
Vanguard Total International Bond Index	10 percent
Vanguard REIT Index	10 percent
Dodge & Cox Income	10 percent
T. Rowe Price Blue Chip Growth	5 percent
Vanguard International Growth	5 percent
Total	100 percent

As I said, those are interesting examples of variations to broad-based investing and may be a bit more exciting to follow and monitor for some investors.

We will now see how various stock and bond mixes have done over the years. The following table from Vanguard shows the average annual return and the worst single-year return of various stock and bond allocations from 1926 until 2015:

Stock/Bond Percentage Percentage	Average Annual Return	Worst Single Year Return
0 percent Stock/100 percent Bonds	5.4 percent	-8.1 percent
20 percent Stocks/80 percent Bonds	6.7 percent	-10.1 percent
40 percent Stocks/60 percent Bonds	7.8 percent	-18.4 percent
60 percent Stocks/40 percent Bonds	8.7 percent	-26.6 percent
80 percent Stocks/20 percent Bonds	9.5 percent	-34.9 percent
100 percent Stocks/0 percent Bonds	10.1 percent	-43.1 percent

Be careful not to do what many investors do, which is to just go for highest historical rate of return. The above data is a bit misleading because if you had been 100 percent invested in the Vanguard Total Stock Market fund, your fund value would have dropped 51 percent over a sixteen-month period beginning with the 2008 recession. Vanguard's Total International Fund was even worse as it plunged 59 percent. The good news is that these funds fully recovered in a bit over three years.

The critical point here is that you should not chase the highest historical yield, which is investing 100 percent into stocks as the volatility is maddening. It seems prudent that the stock-to-bond ratio should be in the range of 60–70 percent stocks and 30–40 percent bonds. Don't be greedy—and remember the proven strategy behind the three-fund approach is to achieve a significant investment return over time while reducing volatility.

I believe the most important thing to take from the historical ups and downs of the markets is to have a solid and clear investment strategy, do not get greedy, and stay the course, knowing full well how emotionally tense it will get in a down market. So take that to heart and invest accordingly. Keep in mind that you will gravitate more toward safety as you get older and reduce your allocation to stocks in favor of fixed income.

There you have it, you Bogleheads and Parrotheads. Perhaps you should unite in the interest of financial security, cheeseburgers in paradise, margaritas, and flip-flops. Seems like a great plan to me.

CHAPTER 6

Robo-Advisers: The Time Has Come—Robot Investing Is Here to Stay

We all knew it was just a matter of time. The digital world affects all aspects of our lives, and robo-advisers have now gone mainstream. It sounds scary, doesn't it? You call your robo-adviser to tell them you want to make some adjustments to your portfolio, and Robo responds in a sophisticated British accent that they have wired all of your money to the Island of Misfit Toys (you might remember that from the Christmas classic *Rudolph*) as part of a new social movement. In all seriousness, technology has actually made investing much easier and more affordable for all levels of investors. I am very upbeat about this exciting development, and I believe it will encourage many new young investors. I believe it will even be popular with advanced investors who have embraced technology.

Let's start this discussion with what robo-investing is not. It is not some crazy computer that is using algorithms and secret formulas to drive frenzied trading strategies. Robo-advisers actually operate much like managed accounts with very low expense ratios (less than 0.4 percent), but additional sophisticated tools are now available to smaller accounts. One of the tools I highly recommend is the *tax-loss harvesting* feature, which sells securities that have lost value to offset capital gains elsewhere in your portfolio. This feature can significantly increase your "after-tax rate of return" because it minimizes your tax burden, which can be problematic with some funds. So the reality is that robo-investing isn't scary at all.

They typically offer managed accounts consisting largely of low-cost index mutual funds—just like the ones discussed in the Bogleheads chapter.

The other good news is that Fidelity, Morgan Stanley, JP Morgan Chase, and Goldman Sachs are all getting into this market. There will soon be a lots of quality options to choose from. There are also a wide range of options for all levels of investors—from beginners with only small amounts to invest to investors who have large amounts in play.

Money magazine has a terrific article in its August 2018 issue that gives a great introduction to Robo-investing, and they did a lot of research for you in terms of how you might proceed. Incidentally, I highly recommend *Money* magazine since their articles are timely and very easy to understand. In the August 2018 article, *Money* examined fifty of the top robo-advisers and came up with their top three: one for beginning investors, one for intermediate investors, and one for advanced investors.

Betterment Digital won the beginner award by offering no minimum balances and many worthy features.

I was also excited to see Schwab Intelligent Advisory Services and Vanguard Personal Advisory Services as the respective winners for intermediate and advanced investors. What I really like about Schwab and Vanguard is that they both combine efficient, low-cost investing with access to real human advisers who are Certified Financial Planners (CFPs). This is a powerful blending of technology with knowledgeable human advisers who can assist with more complex situations as they come up. This really may be the best of all worlds.

It may sound like I have abandoned the Boglehead Three-Fund Portfolio approach in favor of the robo model. Actually, I believe the robo model just takes the Boglehead model a bit further using the same concept of a low-expense, balanced portfolio but adding more sophisticated tools and access to human Certified Financial Planners. It really is just a more advanced version of the Boglehead model.

Before we get too excited about the robo model, we must look at how they perform. Robo-investing is relatively new, and most platforms have only been around for a few years. *Money* magazine focused on the classic balanced investment strategy of 60 percent stocks and 40 percent bonds. They looked at the two-year annualized returns for each robo adviser's balanced portfolio strategy. They then compared them to an investment mix of 60 percent in the S&P stock index and 40 percent in Barclays aggregate bond index. *Money* magazine reported that Betterment's total annualized return for the past two years ended March 31, 2018, was 10.2 percent, Schwab's return was 11.0 percent, and Vanguard's return was 9.6 percent. They all of equaled or exceeded the S&P Stock Index/Barclays Aggregate Bond Index benchmark of 9.6 percent.

Although robo-investing is a relatively new development, the early returns are very competitive—and the stability of your portfolio should be comparable to other proven broad-based investing strategies like the Boglehead model. *Money* magazine also noted that total assets managed by robos doubled to $222 billion last year, and all indications are that it will grow rapidly. Also, all of the big investment houses will be offering their own variations on the robo theme, so you will have many quality firms to choose from.

I believe robo-investing is a sensible investment alternative as long as you keep yourself properly balanced and diversified. The ability to have access to the new tax-harvesting tools and the ability to consult with live Certified Financial Planners make this investment methodology worthy of a hard look for many investors.

CHAPTER 7

So You Want to Be a Day Trader? Don't Even Think about It!

I have had several clients and friends who have attempted to win at the stock day-trading game. Some did it seriously, but kept their real jobs, and others took it on as a full-time undertaking. They all had one thing in common in the end: the "system" beat them every time and just simply wore them out. It is very much like playing blackjack or the slot machine; the house always wins in the long run.

My favorite case study is about a brilliant executive at a large company who was very successful in her own right. She was in her early fifties when she inherited a substantial amount of money from her father. Her father had been a very successful investor over his lifetime, and he earned his fortune the "old-fashioned" way: slow and steady over the long haul.

My friend quit her job, set up a home office, opened multiple trading accounts, and ordered thousands of dollars of investment journals, newsletters, forecasts, and various other investment tools. She considered herself an astute investor and was confident she could master the market as a day trader. She assured me she was going to "crack the system" despite my reservations and cautions.

I was actually very excited to go along for this crazy ride, which would last ten years. What the hell? It wasn't my money, and I was going to have a front-row seat on this interesting adventure. Here is how the numbers game played out over the next decade:

Year	Trades	Cost	Gain (Loss)
2006	$14,344,468	$14,197,546	$146,923
2007	16,673,647	16,577,023	96,624
2008	16,456,161	16,577,244	(101,083)
2009	9,530,033	9,505,331	24,702
2010	72,202,981	72,140,995	61,986
2011	8,250,425	8,295,541	(45,116)
2012	58,768,960	58,783,172	(14,212)
2013	26,205,255	26,196,745	8,510
2014	14,882,979	14,882,853	126
Total	$237,314,909	$237,136,449	$178,460
Average Annual Gain			$19,829

As you can see, this was truly an exercise in investment futility. The following are some critical points and observations I noted during this trading experience:

After $474,451,358 of trades (almost a half billion dollars of buys and sells), millions of transactions, and nine years of intense daily trading, a brilliant person averaged $19,829 in annual investment income.

Ten prime years of an exceptionally intelligent person essentially wasted on day trading. She may disagree with my assessment, but I witnessed firsthand the deep frustration encountered with never being able to master the market, despite intense effort, persistence, and risk tolerance.

It is interesting to note that she began day trading in 2006, when the Dow Jones started at 10,717, peaking on October 11, 2007, at 14,165, for a 32 percent upward run. It is important to point out that October 11, 2007, has been established as the date the Great Recession began as the Dow Jones began its plunge to an ultimate low of 6,443 on March 6, 2009.

That was a historic and painful 54 percent drop. The market then made a steady climb through 2014, ending at 17,823 (an impressive upward move of 276 percent), when my friend threw in the towel. The strong point I am making here is that my friend day-traded through every possible market scenario. She worked through a fairly steady climb from 2005–2007, a complete disaster from 2007–2009, and then a very steady run from 2009–2014. Regardless of the type of market, she just could not figure out how to beat the market despite a frenzy of trading. The clear reality is that no one can win at the day-trading game, regardless of the type of market we are in.

One other interesting takeaway from this experience is that my friend got a bit sucked in by making $146,923 her first year and $96,624 the second year. This was just enough to get her addicted to the gambling phobia of day traders. You may win many times along the way, but eventually, you will bet big the wrong way—and your gains will vanish. It's just like having a bad night at the casino.

Finally, in 2015, she told me she was worn out and was going to go back to a real job and golf a lot more. Of course, I just had to ask, "Why couldn't you beat the market? You spent thousands of dollars on investment research, you were tenacious, and you were willing to risk a ton of money. What went wrong?"

My friend sat back very calmly and said, "No matter how good you are, you cannot consistently pick the upward or downward movement of individuals stocks. Stocks generally go with the flow of the market, just like the tides go up and down. There were companies that I bet on that had a terrific track record, incredible upside, great management, low price-to-earnings ratios, and were totally undervalued. The crazy thing that finally put me away was that all worthy stocks ultimately go with the momentum of the market, whether they should or not. I have decided to go back to investing for the long haul—just like my father did."

So there you have it, all of you prospective day traders. Like life, investing should be a long, steady path void of greed, full of caution, and properly balanced. Do not bet against the house because the house always wins in the end.

Don't despair. In the next chapter, I will let you back into the trading market if you can spare enough money for your own "fun money stock fund." Stay tuned!

CHAPTER 8

Fun Money: Stock Trading if You Have Earned the Right

It is my heartfelt belief that after you have diligently achieved a significant level of investment, you have earned the right to carve out a piece of your portfolio to trade individual stocks. Stock trading is not for everyone, but it does add some spice to your life—and it is better for you than blackjack or slots.

First of all, you are not entitled to be a stock trader until a couple of things have been accomplished. Stock trading should not happen until you have at least six months of living expenses set aside in readily available savings. You also should not set up a trading account until you have at least $200,000 invested in the broad index funds we discussed in previous chapters. After both of these have been accomplished, you have then earned the right to trade stocks with up to 10 percent of your investment portfolio—no more. What the hell, everyone likes to gamble a little bit, and trading in the stock market may be just what the doctor ordered for a little excitement in your life. Many of my clients have done "fun money" stock trading, and they really do have a lot of fun with it. Every one of them thinks (or thought) that they will find those little stock gems that will outperform the market. It might just be the next Apple, Google, Amazon, or—oops—Sports Authority.

Let me first give you some helpful hints on how to go about doing this.

Do not buy any initial public offerings (IPOs) because they are highly volatile, and you may lose a big chunk of your 10 percent in one day.

I suggest purchasing no more than ten stocks and buying them in relatively equal amounts. So if you have $250,000 in qualified investments, you can carve out $25,000 and purchase ten stocks at $2,500 each. You can make the purchases when you feel the timing is right.

Picking and following ten stocks is all that you can reasonably follow and monitor if you are still working. Remember that this is supposed to be fun and exciting, and ten stocks should provide for plenty of analysis and interaction without infringing on your job or family life.

If you are retired and have at least $500,000 in investments, you could amp this up to fifteen or twenty stocks, but I would keep it that.

We all know it is more exciting to bet on a long shot and that you should not base your stock buys on confidential tips from your proctologist or favorite neighborhood bartender. Seriously, try to stick to companies with at least some track record. The most successful picks are usually companies that are emerging and on the verge of breaking out. Part of the fun is that it is your job to find those little stock gems.

Let's now move on to discuss what you can expect based on my experience with lots of clients and investment advisers. Like most intelligent people, we all believe we are better than the average investor and will be successful at picking the best stocks. Unfortunately, the reality is that very few people are good at picking stocks, and if they are successful, it is likely more luck than anything else.

The *Wall Street Journal* on August 18, 2018, reported that they had "revived a long-running contest at the *Journal* where they threw darts at newspaper stock listings to compete against the picks offered by superstar hedge fund managers at the annual Sohn Conference. As you guessed, so far, the darts are winning."

But do not let any of that stop you, my friend! My experience has consistently shown that people don't make much money stock trading, but over time, they don't lose much either. The losers usually just offset the winners. Typically, after a few years of stock trading, most of my clients just got tired of it and moved on to the dog track or online poker.

This much I can guarantee. Stock picking will be a valuable learning experience. Digging into financial statements, reading the *Wall Street Journal*, *Money* magazine, *Barron's*, and the *Motley Fool*, and watching *Mad*

Money's Jim Cramer and Bloomberg TV will be lots of fun. You will also certainly be a big hit at cocktail parties as you talk high finance.

In all seriousness, "fun money" stock trading is good for the mind and soul. It likely won't make you rich or poor, but it will make you smarter and possibly happier. Get after it and show us who the boss is on this financial table. I would put a bundle on green double zero—and go big.

CHAPTER 9

The Catch-and-Release Investment Strategy: A Counterculture Approach

I was reluctant to put this investment strategy into this book because it is nonconventional, is contrary to the traditional stay-the-course investment strategy, and certainly is not for everyone. Actually, the reason I am putting it in is because it is the investment strategy I have personally used and have found success in it over the years, so I thought it needed to be part of the book.

The concept of catch and release is simple. You invest in a mutual fund portfolio consistently over a period of time (the "catch" phase) and then sell the entire mutual fund portfolio and go to cash or CDs prior to the next major market fall (the "release" phase).

This strategy defies the fundamental investment premise that says that you cannot time the market. That principle is absolutely true for individual stocks, but it is not necessarily true for mutual funds. However, you have to be disciplined enough to get out of the market one to two years prior to an inevitable economic downturn and the related substantial market decline (bear market).

Here is how it has worked for me through the recessions of 2001–2002, 2006–2008, and the recession that is on the horizon, in my opinion. I first used the catch-and-release method by just using the Vanguard Windsor Fund and the Vanguard Star Fund, which are balanced funds. I began investing in the Windsor and Star Funds in the 1990s. Here are the annual returns I experienced in the catch phase, which was part of the dot-com craze that spiked the market at the time:

	Windsor Fund	Star Fund
1995	30 percent	29 percent
1996	26 percent	16 percent
1997	22 percent	21 percent
1998	1 percent	12 percent
1999	12 percent	7 percent
2000	16 percent	11 percent
2001	6 percent	0 percent
2002	(22 percent)	(10 percent)

I got very nervous in 1999 when I saw dozens of companies making little or no profit but selling at ridiculous values based on absurd projections. I bailed out of the market in 1999 (the release phase) and went to cash and CDs from 2000 to 2003. I got back into the market after I was convinced we were back to an upside market. I did miss out on the last run-up in early 2000. However, I completely avoided the abrupt market crash that began on March 10, 2000, and continued to fall significantly until the recession ended on October 9, 2002. So my first experience at catch and release worked almost perfectly—certainly with an element of luck—since I did get out just before the crash.

My experience with catch and release was a bit simpler the second time around. I chose to invest only in the Wellington Fund, which is also a balanced fund of approximately 65 percent stocks and 35 percent bonds. I began reinvesting in 2003 over a period of time and experienced the following returns in the next catch phase.

Year	Return
2003	21 percent
2004	11 percent
2005	7 percent
2006	15 percent

In 2006, I got very nervous. I lived in Florida and experienced firsthand the massive speculative investment in residential housing. Many of my clients purchased multiple homes and improved lots with the intent of flipping them for quick profits. I knew things were going to pop as clients began to experience a rapid falloff in demand, so I bailed out of the Wellington Fund in 2006 (the release phase).

The Wellington Fund did return 8 percent in 2007, which I missed out on, but I completely avoided the negative 23 percent crash in 2008. I again was quite successful in timing the crash, but I actually gave myself a better cushion this time and got out well ahead of the market plunge.

My third and final experience with catch and release began in 2009 as I got back into the Wellington Fund after I was comfortable we were back into a bull market. The returns in this catch phase were as follows:

Year	Returns
2009	22 percent
2010	11 percent
2011	4 percent
2012	13 percent
2013	20 percent
2014	10 percent
2015	0 percent
2016	11 percent

I completely bailed out of the market just before the 2016 presidential election and went to cash and CDs. I was convinced Hillary Clinton would win the election and that the market would stagnate or possibly decline rapidly with a Democratic president.

All truth being told, there was another huge factor in my decision. I was sixty-five years old at the time and was not willing to risk any principal ever again in the market. It was time to go permanently to fixed income and live happily ever after.

The crazy thing is that Donald Trump got elected, slashed taxes, and deregulated everything he could. The market loved the huge cash infusion, and the Wellington Fund did 15 percent in 2017 that I missed out on. However, I am sleeping soundly at night and am not the least but concerned with the intense volatility we experienced in 2018. The Dow Jones fell 5.6 percent and the S&P 500 lost 6.2 percent for 2018, and December was the worst December since 1931. I was happy to be on the sidelines.

As I look at the economic landscape, it reminds me of what Yogi Berra once said: "It looks like déjà vu all over again." The economy is poised for a normal cyclical recession as the economy is at an all-time high of ten years of growth, the effects of the tax cuts have leveled off, and the political and world-trade climate is very tenuous and unpredictable.

Regardless, for me, the catch-and-release investment strategy has been successful, but I cannot in good conscience recommend it to others because it is not scientifically sound, and it requires close monitoring and the discipline to get out of the market well before a downturn. All of that is just asking too much of most investors.

I am now happy to be a bystander and protect my principal at all costs. At some point in your life, you just have to decide that security trumps (no pun intended) all other considerations. As the famous business magnate and investor Warren Buffet once said, "Rule number one: Never lose money. Rule number two: Never forget rule number one." Take that to heart, my friends.

CHAPTER 10

The Case for Municipal Bonds— Especially If You Are a Rebel

Muhammad Ali, the most famous boxer of all time, had many problems with the American government and the Internal Revenue Services (IRS).

In fact, in 1966, two years after he won the heavyweight title, he refused to be drafted into the US Army at the height of the Vietnam War. He cited his religious beliefs and opposition to the Vietnam War (officially known as a conscientious objector).

He was eventually found guilty of draft evasion and was stripped of his boxing titles. He appealed the decision to the Supreme Court, who overturned his conviction in 1971.

Ali's troubles with the American government continued well into the 1970s, but this time, his fight was with the IRS over his income taxes. In the middle of his IRS troubles, he proclaimed that one day that he was going to earn $50 to $100 million and put it all into municipal bonds. He would then retire and never have to deal with the IRS again because all of his income would be tax-free.

Unfortunately, Ali had lots of personal and financial problems, and his tax strategy did not work out the way he had hoped. However, the tax strategy is a valid one for certain people, even though it is a bit drastic.

Let me now tell you a similar story that happened to a business acquaintance. He sold his business for millions of dollars, but he was later charged by the American government and spent time at a minimum-security prison. He lost some precious time of his life and was understandably bitter and wanted nothing to do with the American government.

His rebellious answer was to convert most of his investments to municipal bonds, similar to Muhammad Ali's strategy, so he could disconnect from the IRS and American government.

I chose to use these two examples, not to illustrate an antigovernment investment strategy but to actually show how effective a municipal bond portfolio can be for certain investors.

However, before we get too deep into this, it is time for a lesson in managing a municipal bond portfolio. Here is how I suggest you build an effective municipal bond portfolio.

First of all, you should only buy actual bonds and not a bond fund. Investors often misunderstand the fact that bond values go up and down with changes in interest rates. For example, if you bought a bond paying 4 percent interest for $10,000 and interest rates go up to 5 percent a year later, your bond value may drop to say $9,500. This makes sense because why would someone buy a $10,000 bond paying 4 percent when they can get a similar bond that is paying 5 percent. That means you would have to sell your bond at a discount if you chose to do so.

Similarly, if interest rates dropped to 3 percent a year after you bought the bond, your bond would trade at a premium of let's say $10,500. Those are the basic dynamics of the bond world. Individual bond values rise and fall directly with changes in interest rates. It is imperative that you understand this.

It is also important to note that if you buy an actual bond and hold it to maturity, you can absolutely fix your investment yield. In the example above, if you bought a $10,000 bond paying 4 percent, and maturing in five years, your yield will be exactly 4 percent a year if you hold it until it matures.

As I said, you should not buy a municipal bond fund because bond fund values go up and down—and interest rates change. Remember that you have complete control over an individual bond, but you have no control over a municipal bond fund.

You should buy a wide variety of municipal bonds that are actively managed. Diversification in a bond portfolio is essential since every investment carries some risk. I suggest staying in AAA bonds to also reduce risk. Just to be clear, it is possible for a city or a water district to go bankrupt. This risk is slight, and if your portfolio is actively managed, your adviser can sell a bond quickly if a municipality is in financial trouble. This will minimize any bond losses.

You should ladder your bond maturities to reduce interest rate risk and maintain a reasonable amount of liquidity. I would typically ladder or space out your maturities from three to eight years to achieve a targeted overall yield of say 4 percent. I like to stay with maturities of eight years or less. You do not want to get stuck with a 3 percent bond that doesn't mature for fifteen years because if interest rates go to 6 percent, you do not want to miss out on that interest differential.

You should constantly reladder your portfolio as your bonds mature to keep the program intact.

Now let's get back to my rebellious business acquaintance who wanted to disconnect from the IRS and American government. He designed his portfolio to throw off only enough taxable income so that we could shelter with his exemptions and itemized deductions and leave nothing for the IRS. These numbers illustrate how this strategy could work flawlessly:

Year	Tax-Free Municipal Bond Income	Other Income	Tax
1	$601,000	$55,000	$-0-
2	$574,000	$56,000	$-0-
3	$551,000	$58,000	$-0-
4	$675,000	$60,000	$-0-
5	$769,000	$62,000	$-0-

Needless to say, you would need a bunch of municipal bonds to get this result. Obviously, this is not a typical investor from multiple perspectives, but it does illustrate the power of a huge tax loophole for wealthy taxpayers, and it is a realistic strategy for someone who just does not want to pay income taxes for whatever reason.

At this point you are likely saying to yourself, *This is a really interesting case, but how does it apply to more normal people like me?*

This is how it can apply to anyone that is in their peak earning years. The following table shows equivalent taxable yields. In other words, if you had ordinary interest income from CDs, this is the taxable interest rate you would need to get to the equivalent tax-free yield:

Tax-Exempt Yield	Taxable Income Rate of Return Equivalent			
	24% Rate	32% Rate	35% Rate	37% Rate
2.00%	2.63%	2.94%	3.08%	3.17%
3.00%	3.95%	4.41%	4.62%	4.76%
4.00%	5.26%	5.88%	6.15%	6.35%
5.00%	6.58%	7.35%	7.69%	7.94%
6.00%	7.89%	8.82%	9.23%	9.52%

For example, if you had a tax-free bond paying 5 percent and are in the 32 percent tax bracket, you would need a CD paying 7.35 percent to get to the same after-tax yield.

The moral of the story is that municipal bonds can be a very safe and attractive part of your investment portfolio, especially in your peak earning years when you are in a high tax bracket. Muhammad Ali might have been on to something much bigger than boxing.

CHAPTER 11

Why Real Estate Doesn't Make Sense for Most of Us

Real estate for individual investors is very low on my list of recommended investments unless you are a professional in the business or fortunate enough to have the capital to invest in highly attractive commercial real estate.

The following are the realities and myths about real estate that make it one of my least favorite investments for most investors:

Real estate is illiquid.

This happens to be a deal-breaker for me personally. One of the wisest financial advisers I know once said to me, "If you cannot get out of an investment with relative ease, you should pass on it and look to something else."

Speaking from a miserable personal experience, I owned a can't-miss piece of property purchased before the last recession that was virtually impossible to sell during the downturn. That was a painful financial and an emotional experience that I would not wish on anyone.

Real estate is tangible.

That is true. You can see it, touch it, and drive by it every day—and it will never go away. Those are all true statements, but the mere fact that it is real property does not in itself make it a wise investment.

Real estate always holds its value.

This is utter nonsense as real estate values are very cyclical and generally follow the trends of the economy and stock market.

Real estate that is on the water never loses value.

That is another ridiculous myth; almost all real estate is subject to the trends in the economy and market place.

You should leverage and borrow as much as you can against your real estate investments.

There are lots of books out there suggesting that you should buy lots of properties by putting as little of your own money down and use the bank's money for the balance. You get all the appreciation, and the bank just gets a meager interest payment and takes on most of the risk. You get all the upside, and you leverage the investment to make tons of money.

Here is how the story goes. You buy a house for $300,000, putting up $50,000 of your money and borrowing $250,000 from the bank. You fix it up a bit, sell it for $400,000 a year later, and make a profit of $100,000. That is a whopping 200 percent return on your money—and everybody should be doing it, right?

Well, the truth of the matter is that this is possible in a strong up market, but it is usually a disaster in a falling market. Secondly, banks are a lot smarter now, so your equity in the real estate project is going to be at least 20 percent with personal guarantees likely, and you will now have lots of bank oversight.

Most importantly, be prepared for a down market when tenants get into financial problems and may walk away from your lease or force you into a sizeable rent reduction. This cascading effect can end up with you losing your equity through a bank foreclosure and then negotiating your personal guarantee in a period of financial weakness.

Big companies are the best tenants.

Recent history shows that once-stellar tenants like Sports Authority, Circuit City, Sears, and numerous other big-name retailers that have recently gone bankrupt can become nightmare tenants.

Big-company tenants are great in good times, but they can be the worst tenants in bad times if they get into financial trouble. They can be very difficult or impossible to deal with in a downturn, and they may just frustrate you or give you lease-adjustment ultimatums.

I will say that we have many clients who have been successful developing and leasing properties to Walmart, CVS, Walgreens, and UPS. However, these properties are usually only available to large well-capitalized developers. Also, today's great companies may be upside down in five years in today's rapidly changing economic world. So beware. Everything changes as we know, and in the real estate arena, it can change very rapidly.

Build a portfolio of residential rentals.

As far as residential real estate is concerned, "Just don't do it," following the opposite direction of the Nike tagline. It has been the most troublesome and least favorite investment for many of my clients over the years. Residential real estate rentals for high-end properties generally don't make sense because you cannot get the rent that you need to get an acceptable return on your investment. As far the budget side of residential real estate is concerned, I have found this segment of the market to usually be a disaster. Leases are broken often as people literally leave in the night and may strip away anything they can take with them. Low-end tenants are generally not reliable, are often in financial difficulty, and are very needy and demanding on the simplest repairs. Many clients turn their properties over to a management company that takes 15 percent of the gross rent to take some of the problems off of their hands, but this significantly reduces their investment yield in the process.

I know I will get some pushback from successful real estate investors, but years of experience with hundreds of clients has shown real estate to be an investment asset that is the least attractive one. I recognize that large professional developers can be extremely successful, but they have the education, experience, and funding sources to make them successful.

If you feel you must have real estate in your portfolio, I suggest you explore *real estate investment trusts* (REITS) that own hundreds of properties and are professionally managed. They are also publicly traded and do provide an element of liquidity. Personally, I am a bit tepid on REITS, but it is an option to discuss with your financial adviser.

I will close this chapter by sharing the results of two real cases of individuals who are heavily invested in residential real estate. One of them owns twenty-six residential properties, and the other owns twenty-seven residential properties.

The first case had twenty-six rental properties that took in a total $360,500 in gross rents and had $345,000 in rental expenses. The total net income from all of the properties combined was $15,500, or an average of $596 of net income from each property.

The second case had twenty-seven residential properties and took in $281,000 of rental income and had rental expenses of $308,500. That resulted in a net combined rental loss of $27,500, or an average loss of $1,020 per rental property.

This is the best evidence I have as to why residential properties do not make sense for investors who are not real estate professionals. Combining the above two cases, we had a total of fifty-three properties rented that required an immense amount of time and effort and ended up with a net annual loss of about $1,200.

In my opinion, there simply are much better ways to invest your money and time.

CHAPTER 12

Annuities: A Simple Concept Gone Mad

Annuities have been around for a long time and were a reasonable investment alternative until Wall Street made them way too complicated. Unfortunately, embedded in the complexities was the ability to bury significant up-front fees into the products. If no one could understand exactly how they worked because of all of the unnecessary features and options, it was easy to build in high fees. Annuities soon became the product of choice for unscrupulous financial advisers.

As you can tell, I am not a big fan of annuities, but they are making a comeback of sorts, and they seem to be returning to their original purpose. I wasn't going to include them in this book, but I have reconsidered and believe they have a place for certain investors.

Let's start with what an annuity is. In its basic form, it is a type of insurance entitling the investor to a series of annual payments. A basic annuity is a simple contract with an insurance company where you turn over a sum of money in exchange for guaranteed payments over a period of time. The size of your monthly check is determined largely by your age and sex.

For example, a sixty-five-year-old man paying $100,000 for a single premium lifetime annuity would get about $575 per month for the rest of his life. Some people take great comfort in knowing they will get a certain sum each month for as long as they live. There is nothing wrong with this, especially if you live until age ninety. If you only live until age seventy, it was a bad bet since you only would have collected about $35,000. To avoid losing the bet, most people elect for a variation that guarantees a payout of at least fifteen years to you or your spouse. The trade-off is that your monthly payment will be less with this guarantee. I compare this option of betting against the insurance company as like betting against the house in Las Vegas.

By the way, the life expectancy of a sixty-five-year old-male is about eighteen years, so in our above example, he would have been paid about $112,000 for his $100,000 investment if he opted for the fifteen-year guarantee. Certainly not a great return, but research shows that retirees are happier and live longer when they have a guaranteed source of income.

Now we are going to discuss how annuities morphed into some of the most complex financial investments in the marketplace. Annuities are often sold as a way to invest in the market and manage your tax burden. There are several variations of annuities, and I will explain the major ones below:

Immediate Annuities

An immediate annuity is one that begins to pay a monthly income immediately. The insured deposits a specified sum of money with an insurance company, which agrees to pay a monthly income stream for life or for a certain number of years, depending on the annuity option selected.

Single premium immediate annuities may be good investments for those with good health and long life expectancies. Since monthly payments are based on average life expectancy, an immediate annuity is a wise choice if one lives longer than actuarially expected. Immediate annuities offer a convenient way of providing for the income needs of another person, such as an aged parent or a handicapped child.

While no one should put all their money in an immediate annuity, individuals with cash to spare might consider this option for steady income. In general, the size of the monthly check will depend upon age, gender, amount invested, and whether payments cease at death or continue for a specified number of years. A major drawback is that monthly payments may not keep pace with inflation.

Deferred Fixed Annuities

Fixed-rate annuities are insurance contracts designed like retirement plans that work like a CD in a nondeductible IRA. A premium is deposited with an insurance company where the principal earns a tax-deferred yield. The contract can be purchased all at once through single-premium contracts or over time through flexible-premium contracts. At some point, the money is withdrawn—either through periodic payments or in a lump sum—and the tax is paid on the earnings at ordinary tax rates.

Interest is assumed to be withdrawn first and then principal unless an annuity option is selected, and then only a portion of each annuity payment is taxable as ordinary income, as part of it is return of your principal.

Withdrawals of earnings from a deferred annuity before age fifty-nine and a half are treated as ordinary income and are subject to a 10 percent early withdrawal penalty unless the taxpayer is disabled, elects periodic distribution based on life expectancy, or meets other specified exceptions. This latter provision is problematic for me as it severely limits liquidity if you need it.

Deferred-Variable Annuities

A variable annuity bundles a collection of mutual funds into a tax-deferred wrapper that functions much like an IRA. Investors can switch money between funds without triggering taxes, and earnings grow tax-deferred until withdrawn, at which time, regular income tax rates apply. The insurance component of the investment is a guaranteed death benefit. The insurance benefit is guaranteed to pay the value of the retirement account either at death or when the payment period starts, whichever is sooner. Most annuities pay at least the principal amount the customer invested over the years—even if the stock market performance is dismal.

Because of cost and illiquidity, variable annuities are best suited for investors who have maxed out contributions that they can make to IRAs and company retirement plans, who have established liquidity, who intend to leave their money invested for at least a decade, and are willing to accept more risk for potentially higher returns.

While all annuities are tax-deferred, the eventual tax treatment is less favorable than mutual funds because all the earnings on the funds are subject to income tax at ordinary rates. The long-term gains earned on mutual fund holdings are taxed at the often-lower capital-gains tax rate. Also, variable annuities involve insurance expenses, provide no step-up in basis at death, and generally impose early-withdrawal penalties. Because of all the drawbacks noted in this paragraph, I do not recommend variable annuities. Invest in a group of broad-based mutual funds, get the advantage of capital gains, and buy life insurance separately if you need it.

Split Annuities

With a split annuity, an individual purchases two separate annuity contracts that work together to provide a source of income, protection of principal, and a death benefit.

One contract is a single-premium deferred annuity or a CD annuity that earns a guaranteed tax-deferred return for at least five years. The second policy is an immediate annuity that will pay a guaranteed monthly income for five or more years.

The funds used to purchase the two annuities are not split equally because enough must be deposited into the deferred annuity so that at the end of the term of the immediate annuity, the deferred annuity grows to its original face value. After such term, the investor can either purchase another immediate annuity with new funds or begin receiving monthly payments from the deferred annuity.

Needless to say, there are too many factors and way too much confusion going on with split annuities. I recommend staying away from them.

Equity Indexed Annuities

Equity-indexed annuities (EIAs) provide the theoretical upside of investing in stocks without the risk of losing principal. EIAs guarantee that the investment will not lose value when the market goes down. In return, when the market goes up, the investor and the issuing company share the profit. The S&P 500 is commonly used as the benchmark. Every EIA will have a cap and a participation rate. Both affect how they this investment produces its return. The cap is the maximum S&P return recognized by the EIA. The participation rate is the percent of the S&P return credited to the investor's account, which is usually between 50 percent and 80 percent.

This product is a bit more interesting and worthy as you are fully protecting your downside while giving up some of the upside, which may be a reasonable trade-off for some. I believe you can achieve the same result with other investment strategies outside of the annuity world, but these are worth considering—but only with the highest-rated insurance companies.

That is the world of annuities in a nutshell. Only discuss these products with highly reputable investment advisers who only use top-rated insurance companies.

I must confess that this was my least favorable chapter to write because annuities are so complicated that it is almost impossible to simplify them or provide meaningful illustrations. Also, due to their complexity, I have not been able to get a good feel for their performance over time because the results are often difficult to track.

CHAPTER 13

Do I Need a Financial Adviser?
Yes! When the Time Comes

You may have thought from the general tone of this book that I would not recommend a financial adviser. That really is not the case at all. Most people are not overly savvy in the investment arena, and having a trusted adviser help guide you and keep you on track can be a lifetime stress reliever. Keep in mind that you still must insist on a very diverse and balanced investment portfolio that considers your risk tolerance, age, and financial goals. All of the key investment principles set forth in this book absolutely apply—whether or not you have a professional investment adviser.

When you think of it, there are certain key people in your life who go well beyond your family and friends. These key advisers are your CPA, your attorney, your primary care physician, your dentist, your stylist, your priest or rabbi, your personal trainer, your yoga instructor, and, yes, your financial adviser. We all need trusted advisers to give us holistic and practical advice that will benefit us over a lifetime.

Realistically, you are not in need of a full-service financial adviser until you have accumulated six figures in investments. As we have discussed earlier, investors with fewer assets have more options than ever. You can find advisers who charge by the hour or by the financial plan. You can find them through adviser associations like the Garrett Planning Network or the XY Planning Network. These financial advisers will generally work for an agreed-upon fee for a planning arrangement.

Other options discussed earlier include digital investment management services that are now readily available. Robo-advisers are a good option for beginners, those who do not have complicated financial situations, and those who do not need any hand-holding. Many robo-advisers have fees that are in the range of .25 percent of your investment balance, and many do not require minimum balances.

However, as your financial life becomes more complex, you will want to consider a competent full-time human financial adviser. The biggest question you will have when that time comes is: "How do I find a financial adviser who can be trusted and will give me advice that is always in my best interest?" Before you even begin the process, remember that chemistry is critical in this relationship because you have to be honest and transparent with your adviser. Your adviser cannot give you holistic and realistic advice unless they know your goals, desires, and personality. The reality is that you want an adviser who can always relate to your current life stage and financial situation.

Actually seeking out a financial adviser requires embarking on a thorough due diligence process. What could possibly be more important and personal than taking the time to find the right person to share your financial situation, manage your wealth, and work to achieve your lifetime goals and desires?

Getting referrals from your CPA, attorney, trusted business friends, or other successful investors is a good place to start. I generally recommend bigger investment houses or lesser-known investment companies that have been in business for many years and have stood the test of time. The big investment houses have much at stake and generally have strong fiduciary standards in place. Remember it is not very difficult to become a financial adviser since there are not a lot of legal or formal standards that must be met to get into this business at the lowest levels.

Be extremely wary of advisers or companies that guarantee investment returns or play on your emotional, religious, political, ethnic, or other biases that we all have. First and foremost, this about protecting and building your wealth. It is not about nonfinancial matters that unscrupulous advisers often prey on.

Once you have screened a short list of advisers, it is time to go through the personal interview process. The following key considerations should be addressed.

The first big question to ask is "Are you a legal fiduciary?" This has strong legal and ethical significance. This means that the adviser is legally responsible to act in your best interest at all times. This seems obvious, but many broker-dealers operate on a loose "suitability standard." This low standard merely means that the investments they are recommending are "deemed suitable" by them based on their knowledge of your situation.

The short answer is that you should only deal with a "Registered Investment Adviser" (RIA) who is registered with the Securities and Exchange Commission (SEC) or a state securities agency. RIAs are required by law to act as a fiduciary, which legally means they must always act in your best interest. Compare an investment fiduciary to the legal and ethical standards of your attorney, CPA, or trustee of a bank.

The second important question to ask the potential adviser is "Are you a fee-only adviser?" Fee-only means that the adviser is paid by you directly—and only by you. This means that the adviser is not being paid a commission to sell you certain financial products that are lucrative for the adviser.

Also, be careful of fee-based advisers since they often get commissions as well as an investment fee from you. Fee-only advisers and fee-based advisers sound very much alike, but don't be fooled by the semantics. Go for a fee-only adviser!

Lastly, but equally important, seek out an adviser that you are comfortable and compatible with. This relationship can last a lifetime, so be sure you choose someone who understands you, your risk tolerance, your emotions, and your ever-changing lifetime goals.

After you find the adviser you feel comfortable with, schedule an extensive meeting to settle on your formal investment plan. This investment policy and plan should be agreed to in writing.

Shortly after your planning meeting, set up another meeting with your adviser to engage in what I call "investment war games." Investment war games are designed to simulate the conditions you will live through in a difficult and tense down market. I know this sounds crazy, but this will be one of the most important exercises you will ever undertake with your adviser. In fact, it will be of great benefit to both of you.

I will now illustrate how you should play investment war games with your financial adviser. It is easy to say we are going to "stay the course and stick with our investment plan, no matter what," but it is a lot harder to actually live it. So the war game goes like this. You win the lotto in 2005 and have $1 million after taxes. You invest the entire $1 million in June 2005 into the Vanguard Windsor Fund (buying 16,130 shares) at the advice of Tiffany, your financial adviser.

This obviously is a simplification since you would not need Tiffany to simply buy one investment fund. Also, you would never invest only in an equity fund because of the volatility, and doing so would be contrary to the investment principles we have established in this book. Nonetheless, we have done this for illustration purposes only to make an important point.

You and Tiffany meet and are in agreement that since you are forty-three years old, you are going to stay the course and leave your principal and all the earnings in the Windsor Fund until your planned retirement at age fifty-five. We are also going to ignore the positive effect of dividend reinvestments to simplify the illustration.

So here we go. The only rule is that you meet with Tiffany twice a year to discuss your investment progress, and most importantly to "get in the moment" and see if Tiffany can keep you from panic selling. The following table shows your performance history up until you retire in June 2017:

Time Period	Share Price	Value
Jun 2005	$62	$1,000,000
Dec. 2005	$58	$935,510
Jun 2006	$59	$951,670
Dec 2006	$63	$1,016,190
Jun 2007	$64	$1,032,320
Dec 2007	$53	$854,890
Jun 2008	$43	$693,590
Dec 2008	$30	$483,900
Jun 2009	$35	$564,550
Dec 2009	$40	$645,200
Jun 2010	$40	$645,200
Dec 2010	$46	$741,980
Jun 2011	$45	$725,850
Dec 2011	$43	$693,590

Jun 2012	$47	$758,110
Dec 2012	$51	$822,630
Jun 2013	$63	$1,016,190
Dec 2013	$68	$1,096,840
Jun 2014	$72	$1,161,360
Dec 2014	$72	$1,161,360
Jun 2015	$74	$1,193,620
Dec 2015	$65	$1,048,540
Jun 2016	$66	$1,064,580
Dec 2016	$69	$1,112,970
Jun 2017	$76	$1,225,880

As you can see, you get off to a slow start by losing $65,000 in value in your first six months. Tiffany talks you through the current state of the economy and tells you there will be "bumps in the road" but to stay with the plan.

You recover nicely, and your fund is worth $1,032,320 in June 2017, and you are happy to be "back in the black." However, your comfort level falls off rapidly as you find that your fund value drops $177,430 in just six months to $854,890. You are really nervous again and meet with Tiffany again. She says, "No need to panic. It will be okay. We think this is just a temporary downturn."

Six months later, you meet with Tiffany and are frantic. By June 2008, you have lost $306,410—more than 30 percent of your investment. Tiffany has dyed her hair black and calmly tells you that you cannot panic and sell out at what she thinks is the bottom of the market. You both take up smoking and hot yoga to help ease the tension.

Six months later, you call for an emergency meeting since the "sky has fallen." Your investment has crashed to a dismal $483,900, and you have now lost more than half of your $1 million. You are beyond crazy say, "Tiffany, sell now before I lose everything."

Tiffany now has spiked her hair platinum blond, wears sunglasses to work, and puts a lot of stuff in her coffee. She remarkably "talks you off the ledge" and begs you to "hang in there" for one more year. She says, "There are lots of positive signs out there that the Great Recession is over—and things should turn positive."

Fortunately, you agree to stay the course, and within one year, you have had a solid recovery of $161,300. Your fund is now at $645,200. Tiffany quit smoking, now drinks only smoothies, has a new conservative haircut, and has returned to her natural hair color of ebony-black to depict that the market is back in the black.

Your meetings from June 2010 on go very smoothly (except for a little blip late in 2010), and Tiffany buys a bottle of champagne in June 2013 to celebrate that your fund is now $1,016,190. You are weirdly euphoric even though after eight years, you are only back to where you started.

Fortunately, for the next four years, everything is working out nicely as you experience a constant positive incline until you sell out in June 2017 at $1,225,880, just after turning fifty-five. You buy Tiffany a bottle of champagne and decide to buy ten-year US Treasuries at 3.2 percent and leave the market.

Although I have had some fun with this at Tiffany's expense, I am very serious about the importance of this exercise. The extreme pain and helplessness you experience in a down market requires going through this investment war game. In a down market, there is no good news—none! You will hear things like "The market dropped another 486 points today with no end in sight, unemployment is approaching a record high, consumer confidence is at its worst point in thirty-five years, the Federal Reserve doesn't seem to have any answers, the President is blaming the prior administration for this mess, Congress cannot agree on an economic stimulus package, foreclosures and bankruptcies are fast and furious, and M&Ms will no longer make blue or green candies because those are happy colors and nobody is happy anymore."

Seriously, play this out at great length and see if your adviser can use previous written and video coverage during the Great Recession of 2008–2010 to make it as realistic as possible. It will be worth its weight—in gold perhaps.

Good luck in your search for that trusted adviser, and if her name happens to be Tiffany, you know the stars and planets have lined up in your favor.

CHAPTER 14

There Is Always a Storm on the Horizon

Now that we have finished the chapter on financial advisers and investment war games, it may be important to give you a soft warning that a recession is always on the horizon—and investment war games may be sooner than you would like.

I am not trying to be a doomsayer, but I have lived and practiced through multiple painful economic downturns. Although each new generation thinks it has solved economic cycles, I am of the opinion they just cannot be avoided. The pain of a prior recession is largely forgotten after several years, and we tend to make the same mistakes over and over again. It is just human nature.

Rather than telling you why a recession is likely in 2020 or 2021, I am merely going to reflect on the inevitability of an economic downturn based on prior history. We are approaching an economic expansion cycle that will be 120 months long by June 2019. According to the National Bureau of Economic Research, the United States has experienced twelve economic cycles since 1945, and the cycles have averaged sixty months. Only two other cycles—one from 1961–1969 (which lasted 106 months) and the one from 1991–2001 (which lasted 120 months), are even close to our current cycle.

So what I am saying is that we are in the longest economic expansion cycle in the history of modern-era macroeconomics. The historical probability of having a recession in any given year is 15 percent, and given the historical length of this cycle, one can effectively argue that there is a more than 75 percent chance that a downturn will begin sometime in the next twenty-four months. Jeff Kearns, of Bloomberg, wrote in October 2018, "According to a new survey, two-thirds of the business economists in the US expect a recession to begin by the end of 2020." So there you have it—physics and economics agree that what goes up must come down.

There is no need to panic, but I just wanted to point out perhaps that we are overdue for a downturn. However, since we cannot end on a sour note, I quote Vivian Green: "Life isn't about waiting for a storm to pass—it's about learning to dance in the rain." Amen!

CHAPTER 15

Don't Pay Off Your Mortgage? That Advice Is So Terribly Wrong

---

Most financial advisers tell their clients to keep a healthy mortgage to get that great tax deduction and let your money go to work for you. This is poor and misleading advice from both a financial perspective and more so from an emotional perspective. In all my years of dealing with responsible clients, the number one thing that brings them "giddy satisfaction" is paying off their home mortgage once and for all.

Getting yourself out of debt and not beholden to anyone brings immense pleasure and peace to virtually everyone who puts debt behind them. Being debt-free literally sets you free, and the confidence and comfort this brings overwhelmingly outweigh any financial yield differential that is far from guaranteed.

The offsetting argument from the financial community is that if you leave that mortgage money with your broker, they will be able to outpace the cost of your mortgage with investment returns in excess of your mortgage interest rate. Although not obvious to most people, this is essentially buying stocks and bonds on margin with your house as the collateral. Aside from the immeasurable emotional benefit noted above, this financial strategy is also flawed. Let's look at how the numbers play out.

First of all, we are going to dispel the notion that you get a huge tax break from having a mortgage. The 2017 Tax Act really significantly reduced the benefits of a mortgage. The maximum deductible loan is now $750,000, income and property taxes are now limited to a combined $10,000 deduction, and there are no longer *any* miscellaneous itemized deductions. We will now run several scenarios to illustrate my point.

Assume in the first scenario that you have a thirty-year $750,000 mortgage at 5 percent interest. We could run an endless amount of variations, but let's make it simple. Over that thirty-year period, you would pay $699,418 of interest, for an average of $23,314 per year. I am fully aware that there is more interest early in loan and almost none at the end of the loan, but for purposes of this analysis, we will use the average. We will assume a marginal tax rate of 30 percent in all of the scenarios, $2,500 of charitable contributions, and maxing out the $10,000 state and local tax deduction. This is what the tax benefit looks like:

Interest Deduction	$23,314
State and Local Taxes	$10,000
Charities	$2,500
Total Deductions	$35,814
Less Standard Deduction	($24,000)
Itemized Deduction Benefit	$11,814
Tax Savings at 30 percent =	$ 3,544

If you had a $750,000 twenty-year mortgage, your total interest would be $437,920—or annual average interest of $21,896. That is a cumulative interest savings of $261,498. As an aside, I am a firm believer that if you cannot handle the payment on a twenty-year mortgage, you are too highly leveraged and likely overbought in terms of your house. It is okay to use a thirty-year mortgage as a cushion, but plan to pay it off in twenty years. Regardless, if I go through the same calculation as above, your average annual tax savings resulting from the mortgage would be a modest $3,119.

We will now calculate the tax benefit on a more responsible thirty-year mortgage of $500,000, using the same terms. The average annual interest on this loan would be $15,543. The annual net tax benefit on this loan, using the same factors as above, is a paltry $1,213.

If your mortgage is less than $500,000, your net annual tax benefit is virtually *zero*! The evidence is in and irrefutable! The myth of a huge tax benefit flowing from a mortgage has pretty much been obliterated under the 2017 Tax Act.

We will now move on to dispelling the other financial myth of carrying a large mortgage. Your financial adviser may very well say, "Don't pay down your mortgage. You should use that extra cash to invest with me because I will outperform the 5 percent interest rate on your mortgage." The reality is that your adviser cannot absolutely guarantee an annual investment return of more than 5 percent because that would be a statement no one can make.

Let's now look at this from a different perspective. Imagine that if today a bank offered you a fully insured 5 percent certificate of deposit (CD). Most of us would jump all over that offer. Paying down your mortgage is even better than that because the interest on the CD would be taxable, netting you an after-tax return of 3.5 percent. Paying down the mortgage gives you a full after-tax yield of 5 percent, which is the equivalent of a taxable investment return of 7.14 percent—*guaranteed*! What an incredible result and a huge shift in how you should now view your mortgage.

In closing, I realize that virtually all of us take on a house mortgage because we want a home that is ours to live in, and we would like to build some equity. However, reconsider paying down your mortgage much faster than you had ever thought before because the rules of the game have changed. Invest in yourself, and when you have that "mortgage-burning party" to celebrate not paying that monthly payment of $4,026, it will be the happiest financial day of your life.

CHAPTER 16

Perhaps the Biggest Myth of All: Waiting until Age Seventy to Take Social Security

Most financial advisers recommend you wait until age seventy to take Social Security. They make their case by telling you that waiting just four years from age sixty-six until age seventy will increase your Social Security benefit by 30 percent. That, by itself, is a true statement. For example, if you can draw $2,500 at age sixty-six, that will increase to $3,250 if you wait until age seventy. Seems like a financial no-brainer, but it is utter nonsense.

You may not make it until age seventy, never getting to enjoy a single payment after decades of putting money into the system. If you make it to age sixty-five, statistics show there is a fifty-fifty chance you will pass away between ages seventy-two and eighty-eight. However, that also means that 25 percent of the time, you won't make it to age seventy-two. Who in their right mind would take that risk? This may be a bit harsh, but it is a statistical reality.

Financially, the numbers just don't make sense either. By the time you reach age seventy, you would have gotten $120,000 (forty-eight payments of $2,500). Under your financial adviser's premise that you can live comfortably on your other assets until age seventy, the $120,000 in benefits you would have taken at age sixty-six should turn into about $132,000 if invested at 4 percent. If you are still alive at age seventy, you would start taking your $3,250 per month payment. Let's be fair here and assume that your monthly benefit has gone up to $3,400 with Social Security inflation adjustments. Now, let's do the math.

Take the $132,000 that you would have already received if you started your benefits at age sixty-six and divide it by $3,400, which is your increased benefit at age seventy. It will take almost forty months to just break even ($132,000 / $3,400). At that point, You will be almost seventy-four (again assuming you made it until then) to just break even. Factor in the harsh reality that, as you age, your health and mobility (and that of your spouse) will be considerably different than your health and mobility at age sixty-six. That Social Security money that you could have spent on travel or on other lifestyle benefits at age sixty-six may not be nearly as valuable now that you have aged.

So technically, you win the financial game if you make it past age seventy-four, but you will absolutely lose the health and energy game that age will take from you. Financially, and for your lifestyle's sake, take the money and run at the earliest possible date. This is a true case of a bird in the hand is better than two in the bush.

Lastly, the United States is wildly spending at massive deficits approaching $1 trillion a year, even in 2018, which was the best economic year in many years. That kind of deficit spending simply is not sustainable. The Congressional Budget Office reported in January 2019 that the budget deficit will be $900 billion in 2019 and will exceed $1 trillion each year beginning in 2022. There will come a time, and it is sooner than you think, that the American government may be forced to cut your benefits because they are running out of money. Multiple studies also show that the Social Security system will run out of money in the foreseeable future. In fact, the official Social Security Trustee report dated July 13, 2018, stated that Social Security funds will run out of money in 2034, making the argument for taking benefits early even more compelling.

Although this is considered heresy in the financial community, I similarly recommend you take early retirement benefits at age sixty-two if you are earning wages of under $17,640 in 2019—and certainly if you are in bad health. This is the same drill we just went over. In our example, your $2,500 would be reduced to about $2,125 per month by drawing early. That means by the time you reach sixty-six and a half, the full retirement age, you will have already received $140,250 of early Social

Security benefits at a time in your life when you can really use and enjoy it. It will take you almost five years to just break even ($140,250/2500), and you will be seventy-one years old, my friend—and that is a far cry from age sixty-two. Again, don't hesitate to take benefits as soon as you can. Also, I believe early retirement benefits are the best thing going and will likely be one of the first things to go when they redo the Social Security system.

In closing, I believe that significant changes will be made to the Social Security system to keep it solvent. This may include a "financial needs-based system" that will take into account your other income and the amount of your wealth. If the Social Security system determines that you have other assets and income to live on, you may not be eligible for Social Security benefits—or they will be reduced based on your wealth. So I ask you again, Why risk any threat to your Social Security benefits? Take the sure bet and enjoy them as soon as you possibly can! You have earned them!

CHAPTER 17

To Roth or Not to Roth—That Is the Question: The Answer Is Hell No

Roth IRAs came into existence in 1998 as the brainchild of Senator William Roth of Delaware. They are different from a regular IRA by the fact that they are nondeductible but the earnings (if there are any) are tax-free. Again, the big distinction is that you fund them with hard-earned after-tax earnings.

In short, I am not going to mince words here. I just do not like Roth IRAs or Roth IRA conversions, except in very unusual situations that I will discuss later. I do not recommend Roth IRAs for the following reasons.

I have lived by the following cardinal rule my entire career, and it has served me and my clients very well over the years. That cardinal rule is to never pay your taxes before their time. An investment of $5,500 in a deductible IRA will save you about $1,700 in taxes in the 30 percent bracket. A Roth IRA saves you $0 in taxes up front. To say it in another way, a regular deductible IRA of $5,500 only costs you $3,800 in real-time cash because you have sheltered $1,700 in taxes.

I will grant that Roth earnings are tax-free, but they are a disaster if the account loses money. Also, it has been my experience that most people effectively manage their taxable IRAs and take out IRA funds only when they are in much lower tax brackets after retirement. This fact further dilutes the perceived benefit of Roth IRAs. Again, it is my general rule to always push taxes as far into the future as you possibly can and use that tax savings to build wealth. The reality is that if you have a competent tax professional, they will work the tax angles in place at the time you take out your IRA to minimize your tax consequences.

Let's now look at the science and benefits of making annual contributions of $5,500 to a deductible IRA at a 6.5 percent rate of return over thirty years. That modest tax-deductible IRA investment of $5,500 a year turns into $505,941.

Now let's compare that to your nondeductible Roth IRA equivalent, which is only $3,800, because you don't get the $1,700 up-front tax benefit you get from a deductible IRA. After-tax contributions of $3,800 at 6.5 percent for thirty years compounds to $349,559—a whopping $156,382 unfavorable difference. You should take advantage of the tax-deductible IRA and parlay that annual tax savings into a much larger account at the time of your retirement. You can manage the tax consequences way out in the future when you start to make withdrawals.

This same concept works with your 401(k) plan at work. Do not elect the Roth option since it does not make financial sense. If you make a $15,500 contribution to your account each year, it will save you $4,650 in income taxes at a 30 percent rate, for a net out-of-pocket cost of $10,850. Putting that amount in annually for thirty years at a rate of 6.5 percent will generate an account balance of $1,425,833. That is a tidy sum by anyone's standards. Let's compare that to your Roth 401(k) annual contribution amount of $10,850 since you are not getting any tax deduction. That amount invested over thirty years at 6.5 percent gets you an account balance of $998,083, almost a half million dollars less than the deductible 401(k). That is a massive difference, and I believe it dispels any reasonable argument for the Roth 401(k).

I also very much dislike conversions from a regular IRA to a Roth IRA. A real-life example will clearly illustrate why. When Roth IRAs came in during the late nineties, there was a special provision that allowed you to convert your regular IRA to a Roth IRA and pay the taxes over four years without interest. That was very attractive, and a lot of taxpayers fell for the carrot. Here is how it played out for one of my friends. He insisted on converting a $1 million IRA to a Roth IRA in 1998 (contrary to my advice), incurring a tax liability of $320,000 to be paid interest-free in four equal installments of $80,000 per year from 1998 to 2001. Adding fuel to the fire, he invested heavily in the internet/dot-com stock craze just prior to the recession of 2001. Equities dropped more than 30 percent during this recession, and dot-com companies went into a complete free fall. Unfortunately, my friend was heavily invested in these dot-com companies, and his portfolio dropped 60 percent, leaving him with $400,000 in his converted Roth IRA. Ironically, he finished paying his last $80,000 tax installment in 2001 just as his IRA crashed in value. His $1 million converted Roth IRA was now worth $400,000. After you factor in the $320,000 he paid in taxes on the conversion to a Roth, his IRA was worth $80,000 after it was all over. That was a net loss $920,000—or 92 percent of his account. This is a tragic true story and was a massive financial disaster that my friend never recovered from financially or emotionally.

The point I am trying to drill home here is that if you have a loss in a regular IRA, you have at least benefited from a full tax deduction of your principal. That is not the case in a Roth IRA. Prior to the 2017 Tax Act, you had some ability to generate a partial deductible loss from your Roth IRA on your tax return. That option, I believe, is lost entirely with the elimination of all miscellaneous itemized deductions under the 2017 Tax Act, making a Roth IRA even less attractive.

Let me put the Roth conversion in another light. Assume you convert a $100,000 regular IRA to a Roth IRA and pay $30,000 in taxes on the conversion, leaving you with $70,000. You will have to generate a 43 percent investment return on the $70,000 after-tax amount to just get you back to your original $100,000 pretax IRA. This means it would take you almost seven years at a 6 percent annual return just to get back to even. This just doesn't make any financial sense to me.

Roth IRAs may have their place for extremely wealthy individuals with estate tax problems or in weird situations where a taxpayer has huge net operating losses (NOLS) to use, but these situations are few and far between. Stick with regular IRAs since they are a sure thing, and we can plan effectively with them. Successful people often don't need their IRAs to live on in retirement and pass them on to a spouse or children who pay tax on them as they draw on them.

The ultimate tax trick is to leave your regular IRAs to your favorite charities or to your own private foundation, eliminating *all* income and estate taxes. To put this in perspective, assume that you transferred your 401(k) amount of $1,423,855 that we discussed above to an IRA, and then you left this IRA to your favorite charities or your own private foundation. The entire amount would go the charities or your private foundation, and no one would ever pay the embedded income tax of about $500,000. That is an incredible tax trick.

So we end with the question we started with: To Roth or not to Roth? The answer, in my professional opinion, is overwhelmingly not to Roth. Hell no!

CHAPTER 18

It May Be Time to Make a Move—Literally

I have a very easy strategy that will save you 4 percent to 13.3 percent of your annual income for the rest of your life, without earning an additional dollar.

Move, my friend!

If you are flexible and your job skills are mobile, or if you are retired or just reinventing yourself, consider moving to one of the following "no-income-tax" states:

- Alaska
- Florida
- Nevada
- New Hampshire
- South Dakota
- Tennessee
- Texas
- Washington
- Wyoming

These nine wonderful states have no or very minor state income taxes. Let's now see how powerful this state income tax savings can be. Say someone moved in 1988 from my home state of Wisconsin, which had a tax rate of 7.65 percent, to Florida where the tax rate is 0.00 percent. Assume that this person had average annual taxable income of $200,000 through

2018 for purposes of this illustration. Over that thirty-one-year period, saving $12,500 annually in state income taxes, invested at 6 percent, turns into a cool $1,060,021 by 2019. Yes, that means you will have $1 million more working for thirty years in a no-tax state. I realize this is a simple example, but you certainly get the concept of an unsung way to build wealth without an increase in income.

No one can deny that a low-tax state will help build your retirement fund much faster, and the difference can be dramatic by the end of your career. The following table shows the top marginal state income tax rates for 2018 as published by the Tax Foundation. Locate your state, and you can project your own "freebie income tax savings retirement fund." All you have to do is move, which I fully realize involves a lot of factors beyond taxes, but it is something to seriously consider:

California	13.30 percent
Hawaii	11.00 percent
Oregon	9.90 percent
Minnesota	9.85 percent
Iowa	8.98 percent
New Jersey	8.97 percent
District of Columbia	8.95 percent
New York	8.82 percent
Wisconsin	7.65 percent
Idaho	7.40 percent
Maine	7.15 percent
South Carolina	7.00 percent
Connecticut	6.99 percent
Arkansas	6.90 percent
Montana	6.90 percent
Nebraska	6.84 percent
Delaware	6.60 percent
West Virginia	6.50 percent
Georgia	6.00 percent
Kentucky	6.00 percent
Louisiana	6.00 percent

Rhode Island	5.99 percent
Missouri	5.90 percent
Maryland	5.75 percent
Virginia	5.75 percent
Kansas	5.70 percent
North Carolina	5.50 percent
Massachusetts	5.10 percent
Alabama	5.00 percent
Ohio	5.00 percent
Oklahoma	5.00 percent
Mississippi	5.00 percent
Utah	5.00 percent
Illinois	4.95 percent
New Mexico	4.90 percent
Colorado	4.63 percent
Arizona	4.54 percent
Michigan	4.25 percent
Indiana	3.23 percent
Pennsylvania	3.07 percent
North Dakota	2.90 percent

Incidentally, the tax motive to move to a no-income-tax state is bigger than it has ever been because of the huge negative effect of the Tax Cuts and Jobs Act of 2017. Taxpayers now can deduct no more than $10,000 of your combined state income taxes, sales tax, and property taxes. This is an absolute nightmare for those poor souls in high-tax states since they may see no personal tax benefits from the 2017 tax law, and many of them will actually have a tax increase.

Let's throw in a bonus round here on the financial advantages of moving to a "low-cost state." This is different from a no-income-tax state, although they often go hand in hand. A low-cost state is exactly what it says. It is a state where your cost of living is considerably lower than most other states. Assume that you have built a savings retirement fund of $1 million, regardless of where you live. *Money* magazine, in the summer of 2018, published a study that showed how long a savings of $1 million would last in a particular state. This is a huge eye-opener. The following are the *Money* magazine findings:

How Long $1 Million of Savings Will Last in Every State:

More Than Twenty-Four Years

- Indiana
- Oklahoma
- Alabama
- Kansas
- Texas
- Tennessee
- Georgia
- Arkansas
- Michigan
- Mississippi
- Missouri

Between Twenty and Twenty-Four Years

- Arizona
- Colorado
- Delaware
- Florida
- Idaho
- Illinois
- Iowa
- Kentucky
- Louisiana
- Minnesota
- Montana
- Nebraska
- Nevada
- New Mexico
- North Carolina
- North Dakota
- Ohio
- Pennsylvania
- South Carolina
- South Dakota
- Utah
- Virginia
- Washington
- West Virginia
- Wisconsin
- Wyoming

Less Than Twenty Years

- Alaska
- California
- Connecticut
- DC
- Hawaii
- Maine
- Maryland
- Massachusetts

- New Hampshire
- New Jersey
- New York

- Oregon
- Rhode Island
- Vermont

Another way to look at this is that if you move from one of the fourteen highest-cost states to one of the eleven lowest-cost states at time of retirement or a lifestyle change, your $1 million effectively turns into $1.2 million as soon as you cross the border to that low-cost state. You are now certainly asking, "How did you get from $1 million to $1.2 million by just crossing a state border?" Look at it this way. If you have $1 million and live in a high-cost state like New York, it will last twenty years according to *Money* magazine. By doing the math, that means in New York, you would be spending $50,000 a year assuming inflation and investment returns cancel each other out. By moving to a low-cost state like Texas or Tennessee, that $1 million will last twenty-five years, which means you will only have to spend $40,000 per year. That $40,000 for the extra five years effectively gets you to the equivalent of $1.2 million. That is how I got there. If you prefer to move to my new home state of Florida, you will get similar results.

Let me say it one other away to slam the idea home. If you are sixty-six when you retire in New York with $1 million, it will last you until you are eighty-six. If you retire in Texas, Tennessee, or Florida, it will last you until you are ninety-one.

Now here is how you double down. You move to a no-income-tax state that is also a low-cost-of-living state, and that combination of financial factors can have a staggering upward impact on your retirement nest egg.

I realize this is pretty crazy stuff that you hadn't thought about before, but it is certainly something to think about and take seriously. Also, moving can be very exciting with a new climate, food traditions, geography, music, people, and fun.

CHAPTER 19

Bonus Round: How to Save Thousands without Working or Sacrificing Anything

On the huge mistake side, never buy an investment that is so complex you do not understand it, especially if it is illiquid. Part of the charm and attraction of obscure investments is that they are designed to be "exclusive" and complicated to give off an aura that these are only available to a select few. This could be anything from investing in a movie, an intriguing technology development, or something as mundane as buying up a group of assisted-living facilities or oil and gas wells. If you don't have a full understanding of how the investment operates, and exactly how the income will flow, stay away! Don't be fooled by syndicators who promote complex investment opportunities as far superior to more traditional alternatives; they almost always rely on "projections and pro formas" to lure you in.

Stick with easy-to-understand investments that have stood the test of time. This is the most glaring and costly mistake I have seen clients make over the years. Everyone wants that "silver bullet" or "secret sauce" that will get them rich quick. Some of my most intelligent clients put substantial amounts of money into can't-miss investment strategies—only to find out they just bought a shiny object that was not made of gold but of fool's gold.

We have all heard the saying that there is no such thing as a free lunch, especially if it is at a fancy and expensive restaurant. You may think you can resist the *investment push*, but I have seen many "invulnerable clients" fall for the free lunch in exchange for a poor or worthless investment. That free lunch usually ends up costing thousands of dollars and lots of emotional turmoil. A $10,000 bust is worth two hundred $50 lunches—so just pay for your own damn lunch.

Stay away from thirty-day free trials, especially if they require a credit card. These often turn into an automatic monthly billing that goes on indefinitely. By design, these arrangements are difficult to cancel, and our human nature is to let things slide as we just don't get around to canceling these types of things until you have spent way more than you ever intended. Do your due diligence up front. After careful, analytical thought, you should then decide whether or not you need the product or service. Don't be lured into the free-month thing as it rarely ends there.

Similar to the thirty-day-free-trial trap, stay away from limited-time offers since this is a very effective sales technique. I recall looking at a new car I really wanted; it was just before Christmas. The charming salesperson had me going, and then he laid it on me. "There are only twelve hours left in the pre-Christmas sale before I can no longer sell you the car at cost." The incredible holiday sale was rapidly coming to a close, and I had to make a decision. Unfortunately, I did not pull the trigger—and I missed the sale.

Remarkably, three weeks later, in early January, I returned to the dealership to see what was available. Yes, you guessed it. The car I so desperately wanted was still available, and it was now selling for $2,200 less than during the holiday sale. As you might expect, January is a horrible month for auto sales, so it is a good time to buy when nobody is in the market.

Salespeople are very good at creating urgency, but do not fall for it. There is *always* a similar or better deal on the horizon. Limited-time offers trigger your buying urge before your internal logic catches up with you.

Never buy anything that common sense tells you is too good to be true. A free phone always comes with a long-term contract and that time-sensitive 50 percent-off vacation or cruise never quite plays out that way. That totally free five-day vacation at a time-share resort will probably be the most miserable five days of your life—as you try desperately to avoid those intense sales presentations.

So the next time you are offered something that is too good to be true, walk away because it almost always is.

It is a crazy thing, but studies show that autopay bills are 5–10 percent higher than bills paid directly by check. Why is that, you wonder? It is very simple. We just don't think about the cable, utility, or other bills much when they are automatically deducted. When bills are paid automatically, you don't pay as much attention to energy usage, cable creep, the monthly music service, the upgraded app of choice, and on and on.

To put a personal spin on this, our football group recently paid $1,200 in cash for four scalped Green Bay Packers tickets. After painfully peeling off twelve crisp hundred-dollar bills, I was taken back by the significance of the transaction. The experience just didn't match up—even for a cult Packers fan. Even worse, if I had bought the tickets on SeatGeek or Ticketmaster, with the fees, it would have been more like $400 per ticket. However, it would not have been nearly as painful as peeling off twelve crisp Benjamin Franklins because it would only show up as a one little line item on my credit card bill.

Avoid like the flu: Black Friday, Cyber Monday, Amazon Prime Day, and all the other major shopping-hype days. They will suck you into buying last year's models, overstocks, and items that just did not sell. More dangerous is the way they lead you into buying pop-up items, sucking you into buying multiple items you had not even considered because you got caught up in the frenzied marketing moment. Take a pause and buy things as you need them—when you have a clear head to make sensible decisions without all the hype.

Do not buy anything after or while drinking alcohol or smoking medical marijuana. Especially don't buy things on the internet at night— or anytime, for that matter—if you are in the party mood. This should be self-evident, but all the normal safeguards that sobriety brings are remarkably lost while under the influence. Everything you see that seems to be a necessity while you are in the mood will vanish the next morning as buyer's remorse sets in. This strategy will literally save you thousands of dollars of wasted spending over time. How do I know? Perhaps from experience?

As I close, I have to tell you that if you have been a successful saver over your lifetime, and have a solid financial cushion, you have earned the right to be a bit frivolous. You needn't have to ask if you can go anywhere or buy anything. It is up to you to decide or care how you will feel afterward. Anyway, what's wrong with those delightful, impulsive purchases after you have worked a lifetime for the right and privilege of spending your money as you see fit? Laissez les bon temps rouler!

CHAPTER 20

Does College Pay? It Certainly Does—but Choose with Care

Providing for a child's education is one of the primary responsibilities of a parent, but it can be a significant financial burden. Is college worth all that money and time? Where is the best value for my college dollar? This chapter will help answer those questions and hopefully a bit more.

But before we get started, it is important to say that from my experience of hiring and working with hundreds of employees, education is a starting point and may get you in the door, but performance is the only thing that matters in the end.

I have not seen any discernable difference in the success or failure of colleagues because of where they went to college. If you attended a solid four-year college (and perhaps beyond) and applied yourself, the success rate in my experience is pretty consistent, regardless of where you went to college. It has also been my experience in working with hundreds of private businesses that they are all open to discussing job opportunities with qualified candidates from all respectable colleges.

However, I have to admit that it is no secret that the elite schools are more connected to many of the best jobs in the country because of their deep social and cultural ties to Wall Street. The stark reality is that those connections are powerful and meaningful to big business, and you just have to accept that they lean heavily toward big-name schools.

Also, elite colleges like Harvard, Yale, Stanford, Princeton, and Duke have acceptance rates of between 5 percent and 12 percent, so your chances of getting in are pretty slim without any "legacy student" status. Legacy students are typically students who have considerable social status, strong alumni connections, and usually attend elite preparatory schools that are closely linked to the elite colleges. Regardless, don't let this stop you from applying. These colleges are under pressure to open their enrollments more to nonelite students, and it appears that trends are moving in that direction.

First of all, college absolutely does pay! The Federal Reserve Bank of Saint Louis reported the following in a study released in April of 2018:

- Families headed by a non-college-graduate earned only 44 percent of what the median college-graduate family earned.
- More revealing was that the median non-college-graduate family has only 18 percent as much wealth as the median college-grad family.
- The median college-graduate income in 2016 was approximately $92,000.
- The wealth of a median college-graduate family was $291,000 in 2016, compared to the wealth of a nongraduate family of $54,000.

To put this in terms of investment returns, the Federal Reserve of New York reported in 2018 that the return on earnings of a bachelor's degree remains high, averaging 15 percent over the past decade. Put somewhat differently, the return on an undergraduate education is more than double the average annual return of the stock market since 1950 and five times the return on bonds for the same period.

Furthermore, a 2015 study by Georgetown University found that, on average, workers with a bachelor's degree earn $1 million more over their lifetimes than those with only a high school diploma.

Although college isn't for everyone, there is clear evidence that from a financial perspective, a college degree is worth the investment. However, the problem with much of the evidence is that the data uses averages and trends, and we all know that the cost and quality of colleges differ drastically. That is what we are about to sort out. How and where to make that college investment is the mystery we are about to unravel. I believe that what you are about to read is going to really open some eyes and hopefully some doors.

Before we go too far, we must recognize that college graduates are smothered with $1.4 trillion of college debt, putting them in a difficult financial situation even before they have a job. The class of 2017 average graduate took out student loans of $39,400, delaying or impeding their ability to buy a home, get married, or have children. If you graduated in education, the arts, or social work, your average salary was about $39,000, according to that same Georgetown University study. So my first recommendation is to choose your college not only by its name or reputation, but by how that institution offers a price tag with minimal debt obligations. So the ultimate question is just like every other purchase you make. Which college gives you the best bang for your buck? You may be surprised by these results.

Let me start out by giving you my own personal college experience. My father was a teacher and one hell of a high school basketball coach. He was actually sort of famous in Wisconsin Valley Conference history. The unfortunate part is that his job paid terribly. My mother had seven children and was a stay-at-home mother just trying to survive with four delightful boys and three whiners (my sisters). My mother once tried to fool us by mixing powdered milk with real milk to save money. That experiment did not work—not for even for a day—since growing Wisconsin boys know real milk from imposters. Needless to say, my parents did not have a big old juicy college fund for me when I turned eighteen, but they did raise me in a warm, loving, and safe household—more than anyone could ever ask. However, college was on my own.

As luck and good fortune would have it, I was offered a scholarship to Loyola University in New Orleans. For someone who had never left the state of Wisconsin, I was all in and went to Loyola sight unseen. It had never occurred to me that someone with limited financial means could go to an expensive private college. This is the first college myth I want to dispel. Loyola, like most private institutions, has a sizable endowment fund to provide scholarships to qualified students. After getting to know the financial aid people at Loyola, they told me that most of their students come from well-to-do families who did not need or expect financial assistance. This same situation exists at Harvard, Duke, Princeton, Berea College,

Wisconsin, Michigan, UCLA, LSU, Alverno College, and on and on. The reality is that if you are a highly qualified student of modest means, you can go to virtually any college you want as they all have substantial amounts of financial assistance available for exceptional students. However, as we know, the elite colleges in this country are very difficult to get into regardless of your qualifications if you are not a legacy student. My answer to that is make lots of noise and be ridiculously persistent. Break the door down if you have to.

It is now time to get into the details as to where you should consider investing your college dollars. The *Wall Street Journal* (WSJ) released its top rankings of American colleges on September 6, 2018. This is an exceptional analysis from the premier financial publication in the world. There are more than three thousand four-year colleges in the United States. The *WSJ* analyzed approximately one thousand of these colleges and rated the top five hundred. It is safe to say that if you see one of your prospective colleges on this list, it is worthy of your consideration.

> The *WSJ* rankings emphasize how well a college will prepare students for life after graduation. The overall ranking is based on 15 factors across four categories: Forty percent of each school's overall score comes from student outcomes, including a measure of graduate salaries, 30 percent from the school's academic resources, 20 percent from how well it engages its students, and 10 percent from the diversity of its students and staff.

Since this book is about finance, we are going to focus on overall rank but with a heavy emphasis on the total net average annual cost, projected salary, and the default rate on student loans. For private schools, net average cost is the total cost to attend, including room and board, minus the average total grant and scholarship aid received. For public colleges, the net average cost is the published in-state tuition and room and board figure.

Projected salaries are the average salary after graduating from college. The default rate shows the percentage of people in default on their student loans.

Since we are focusing on value, we will start with the *WSJ's* top ten best values based on overall score and average net total price.

Value Rank	WSJ Ten Best Values	Average Net Cost	Projected Salary	Default Rate	Overall Rank	Acceptance Rate
1	Berea College—Berea, KY	2,862	38,200	6.0	230	35 percent
2	University of North Carolina—Chapel Hill	10,077	51,833	1.8	37	24 percent
3	University of Washington—Seattle	10,068	53,533	2.7	61	45 percent
4	Purdue University—West Lafayette	11,693	53,967	2.5	43	57 percent
5	UCLA	14,236	59,167	2.1	25	19 percent
6	Harvard University	16,205	91,200	0.7	1	6 percent
7	University of Illinois—Chicago	11,571	51,633	2.7	13	77 percent
8	Georgia Tech	13,340	74,767	1.3	60	23 percent
9	Rutgers University—Newark	10,771	55,233	3.4	231	64 percent
10	Stanford University	16,695	84,200	1.1	6	5 percent

I am now going to extract my own analytics from the *WSJ* survey and show you sixteen of the top seventy-five colleges, rated in order by average total net cost:

	Least Cost Rank	Overall Rank	Average Net Cost	Projected Salary	Default Rate	Public Private	Acceptance Rate
University of Washington— Seattle	1	60	$10,068	$53,533	2.7	Public	45 percent
University of North Carolina— Chapel Hill	2	37	$10,077	$51,833	1.8	Public	24 percent
Purdue University— W. Lafayette	3	43	$11,693	$53,967	2.5	Public	57 percent
Georgia Tech	4	59	$13,340	$74,767	1.3	Public	23 percent
UCLA	5	25	$14,236	$59,167	2.1	Public	19 percent
University of Florida	6	73	$14,761	$51,883	2.7	Public	42 percent
University of Wisconsin	7	66	$15,874	$52,267	1.5	Public	54 percent
University of Virginia	8	51	$15,945	$59,800	1.3	Public	27 percent
University of Michigan	9	28	$16,107	$58,647	1.3	Public	33 percent
Harvard University	10	1	$16,205	$91,200	0.7	Private	6 percent
University of Texas	11	62	$16,010	$53,567	2.5	Private	36 percent
University of Illinois	12	48	$16,683	$56,933	1.8	Public	52 percent
Stanford University	13	6	$16,695	$84,200	1.1	Private	5 percent
Princeton University	14	9	$17,730	$77,833	2.9	Private	8 percent
Yale University	15	3	$18,319	$74,467	1.5	Private	7 percent
Duke University	16	7	$19,950	$77,100	.07	Private	12 percent

I came to some really surprising conclusions.

Harvard's website states that tuition, fees room and board will cost a student $67,580 per year for 2018–2019. That is the actual cost if you are financially well-off. That number probably does not surprise any of us.

It was a complete surprise that you can go to the most prestigious college in America for an average total annual net cost of $16,205, or $64,820 for a four-year degree. You combine that with a projected postgraduate annual salary of $91,200, and you wonder why everyone doesn't go to Harvard. Well, we all know that very few of us can get into Harvard, but the critical point is that Harvard and most great institutions are surprisingly affordable if you are a qualified student and are fortunate enough to get in.

Unfortunately, most of us would not even consider applying to many colleges because of the myth that they are not affordable for most students. Hopefully, we have dispelled the myth that prestigious colleges are not out of reach for intelligent students of modest financial means. So go ahead and break the mold—and blast your way into the Harvard Crimson or wherever you choose to go.

Before moving on, we must explain how you get from Harvard's published cost of $67,580 to the *WSJ* total average net cost of $16,205, a hefty difference of $51,375. Who pays that huge dollar difference for that deserving student? There are several possible sources, but the most obvious source is Harvard's $37 billion academic endowment—the largest in the world. Harvard, like most colleges, has substantial academic endowment funds available to assist qualified students with limited financial resources.

Another powerful revelation in the *WSJ* survey is that the top three public colleges by average cost (University of Washington, University of North Carolina, and Purdue University) are $10,613 per year, or $42,452 for a bachelor's degree. That is in exchange for an average postgraduation salary of $53,111. How impressive is that? In fact, of the eleven public colleges I selected out of the top seventy-five institutions, the total average cost to attend these colleges is only $14,604 per year, or $58,416 for a four-year bachelor's degree. Not a bad investment for a projected annual salary of $53,111.

Let's now get an inside look at the total average net annual cost of Harvard, Yale, Stanford, Duke, and Princeton—the first-, third-, sixth-, seventh-, and ninth-highest-rated colleges in the entire survey. That total net average cost is $17,780 or $71,120 for a bachelor's degree from these institutions. That investment is in exchange for a projected average annual salary of $80,813.

After writing much of this, I got the uncomfortable sense that my readers may feel I am too focused on the top colleges in America and not the Main Street local colleges most of us attend. That really was not my intent at all. My goal was to simply point out to students, parents, and grandparents that you should open your horizons and consider going to the college of your dreams since it is more affordable than you think.

Let's now look into Main Street USA Colleges and their affordability. The following is the College Board's annual survey of the "in-state tuition and fees for all fifty states." Keep in mind that these cost numbers are before any financial assistance, and they do not include room and board, which runs about $11,000 per year for public colleges.

In-State Tuition Cost and Fees for 2017–2018 before Financial Aid

Rank	State	Tuition Cost		Rank	State	Tuition Cost
1	Wyoming	$ 5,220		26	Maryland	$ 9,580
2	Florida	$ 6,360		27	California	$ 9,680
3	Utah	$ 6,790		28	Tennessee	$ 9,790
4	Montana	$ 6,910		29	Texas	$ 9,840
5	New Mexico	$ 6,920		30	Maine	$ 9,970
6	Idaho	$ 7,250		31	Kentucky	$ 10,300
7	Nevada	$ 7,270		32	Oregon	$ 10,360
8	North Carolina	$ 7,380		33	Ohio	$ 10,510
9	Alaska	$ 7,440		34	Alabama	$ 10,530
10	West Virginia	$ 7,890		35	Hawaii	$ 10,660
11	New York	$ 7,940		36	Colorado	$ 10,800
12	Mississippi	$ 7,990		37	Arizona	$ 11,220
13	North Dakota	$ 8,200		38	Minnesota	$ 11,300
14	Nebraska	$ 8,270		39	Rhode Island	$ 12,230
15	South Dakota	$ 8,450		40	Delaware	$ 12,270
16	Oklahoma	$ 8,460		41	Connecticut	$ 12,390

17	Arkansas	$ 8,550		42	South Carolina	$ 12,610
18	Georgia	$ 8,570		43	Massachusetts	$ 12,730
19	Iowa	$ 8,760		44	Virginia	$ 12,820
20	Missouri	$ 8,870		45	Michigan	$ 12,930
21	Wisconsin	$ 8,960		46	Illinois	$ 13,620
22	Kansas	$ 9,230		47	New Jersey	$ 13,870
23	Louisiana	$ 9,300		48	Pennsylvania	$ 14,440
24	Indiana	$ 9,360		49	Vermont	$ 16,040
25	Washington	$ 9,480		50	New Hampshire	$ 16,070

Keep in mind that the tuition and fee numbers reported are before any financial assistance. Financial aid is readily available in all of the states, based on the quality of the student and financial need. Since we do not have access to how much average financial aid goes to a student, full comparative analysis is not possible. However, I can say with confidence that the average net assistance per student at all public colleges is significant. We will have to leave it with the premise that college is affordable in this country at all levels, but extensive research and analysis is necessary to get your best value.

Spend the time and effort necessary to achieve the best outcome possible because this is going to be the most important investment of your life. The key is to find a college you can afford and be acutely aware of what your salary expectations are in the course of study you have chosen. Also, be very cautious of going into great debt to get a college degree as student loans are now haunting millions of graduates. There will be more on that subject in the next chapter.

Finally, before we finish this chapter, it is important to note that technology is drastically changing the cost and availability of a quality college education. In 2014, Georgia Tech launched a completely online master's of science in computer technology. Georgia Tech is a top-ten college of computing. It was offered in collaboration with Udacity and AT&T with an annual cost of about $7,000 per year compared to $45,000 for on-campus students. There are more than two thousand students enrolled, and its early graduation results show that online students equaled or exceeded the accomplishments of traditional students.

The point is that the traditional college experience is rapidly changing, giving students in all areas of the country, urban and rural, affordable options that were not available even a few years ago. Purdue University just launched Purdue University Global, an online degree program for working adults. Suffice it to say that the college world is permanently changing for the better. College is now coming to you instead of you having to go to college.

It is now time to go on to the next chapter, which will focus on the available tools to fund that college degree. See you there.

CHAPTER 21

Funding the Quest for a College Degree

Paying for college is one of the biggest financial obligations that students, parents, and grandparents will ever face. Doing it the right way requires a lot of planning and the benefit of time. If you literally start saving shortly after your child is born, this financial obligation will be much easier to tackle.

Also, for a little lagniappe early in this chapter, I will give you the best trick ever to help fund your kids' educations. Your parents, grandparents, and close relatives are very vulnerable after a child is born. Tell them early that you are planning to start funding for little Noah's education soon after birth, and any gifts to his college fund would be much appreciated by little Noah and his parents. Don't hesitate to ask Mom and Dad, and Grammy and Papa, and maybe even rich Aunt Matilda if they would like to help a little to fund Noah's college education.

Show them the actual prepaid college plan you are thinking about and tell them you can manage to put in about $100 per month—and were wondering if they might want to match that—for precious little Noah. I am telling you that this trick works; all you have to do is ask. You just might get considerably more than you thought, and if they say no, just tell them little Noah is now off-limits. Seriously, this is worth a simple ask, and it almost always works.

It is now time to discuss the best college funding options available out there. Optimum college planning often involves a combination of the following strategies:

State Prepaid Plans (Florida in This Case)

This is my favorite college-savings strategy for the following reasons:

- They are simple and understandable.
- They are affordable and can be paid monthly.
- Your investment is guaranteed by the state so you will never lose any of your investment.
- You do not have to worry about the stock market or the rising cost of tuition and student housing (if you choose this option).
- These plans allow for a variety of options that include funding for one to four years of tuition and similarly funding for student housing.
- These plans can be applied to other colleges nationwide—public or private—at the same rate they would pay a Florida school.
- If you move out of Florida, your child can still use the plan as if your child was an in-state student.
- These plans are transferable to another eligible family member if this child does not go to college.
- If your child gets a scholarship, you can get a refund, apply it toward lodging, or transfer it to another child.
- Most important, my clients have gotten great emotional satisfaction knowing that they have funded a large part of their children's education to great colleges located conveniently in the state that they know and love.

Let me use the Florida Prepaid Program as to illustrate the possible funding arrangements. The following are just some of the options available in Florida if you enroll in the program when the child is a newborn:

	216 Months	60 Months	One Payment
Four-Year College Plan	$120	$363	$18,924
Four-Year University Plan	$186	$565	$29,442
One-Year Dormitory Plan	$48	$145	$ 7,577

Florida has twelve state universities and twenty-eight state colleges. The state colleges have fewer academic offerings and no gigantic football stadiums, and they are less expensive to fund.

The inherent interest rate Florida is using in these calculations appears to be 4 percent since that is what they have built into their optional payment plans. In other words, if you use the monthly or sixty-month options, they are charging you 4 percent interest to do so, which is a pretty good deal.

Section 529 Savings Plans

My second favorite college-funding plan is the Section 529 savings plan. These are savings plans that allow earnings to be totally tax-free if the principal and earnings in the plan are spent on qualified educational expenses.

There are two basic strategies to use: a designed simple approach to savings or a customized savings approach.

I prefer the predesigned approach that uses a target date plan that is set up to adjust the mix of your investments as your child approaches college age. This is one simple fund and is best for parents who prefer simplicity and are not overly savvy in financial matters. These are known as "age-based/years-to-enrollment portfolios." It sounds complicated, but it really is just a portfolio that allocates your contributions to a "blended-equity and fixed-income fund" based on your child's number of years until college enrollment. The younger your child is, the higher the percentage is that is invested in stocks. As your child approaches college enrollment, the percentage invested is stocks decreases, and the percentage invested in fixed-income funds increases.

The goal of this transition is to take on less risk as your child approaches the time when the portfolio will be used for their education. This savings option is very similar to *target-date retirement funds*, which operate in a similar fashion. As you approach your *retirement target date*, the fund moves more heavily into fixed-income funds.

The *customized-funding approach* may be best left to your financial adviser. However, Florida has six respectable investment options in their Section 529 offerings. They include a more aggressive blended-stock-only portfolio, a balanced portfolio of 50 percent stocks and 50 percent fixed income, a 100 percent fixed-income fund, and an ultraconservative money-market fund. These are all reasonable options, depending on your risk tolerance, but I would not recommend the 100 percent stock fund. If Miserable Melissa is entering college at the time of a big stock downturn, you could end up with less money than you put in, and Miserable Melissa may end up staying at home and torturing her parents indefinitely.

Gifts to Minor Act Personal Savings Plan

This next option can work independently of other college-funding strategies, but it works best in conjunction with one of the plans discussed above. This strategy is simply gifting money to a child under the *Uniform Gift to Minors Act* (UGMA). An account is set up in the child's name and Social Security number and is taxed at the child's rate. The favorable income tax play is the key to this strategy. However, managing the "kiddie tax" is critical. Here is how it works.

Mad Dog Mikey or Senseless Susie receive cash gifts from time to time from their parents, grandparents, friends, and relatives. Their parents religiously put all of these cash gifts into their respective savings accounts for college. Under the 2017 Tax Law, a child can earn up to $12,000 a year working for McDonald's, Chick-fil-A, or Nick's Organic Fast Food. Parents should see that some of that money gets into their college savings account, and this money should be invested conservatively.

I have determined that just under $5,000 of unearned income is the optimum point where the tax will only be about $500 on these earnings—well below what the parents would pay. Perhaps this is a bit optimistic, but it means a child could have about $170,000 in a CD paying 3 percent to hit the $5,000 optimum point of unearned income. Whatever the amount is, this should serve as part of the overall college-funding plan.

Now for the bad news, my friends. Accounts under the UGMA become the child's at age eighteen. Prior to age eighteen, the parents act as legal custodians. As we all know, turning over any money to an eighteen-year-old is a crazy thing to do—so you have to control these accounts. Keep your children as much in the dark as you can. Be sure only you have access to the bank or investment statements and that any mail comes to you. When the time comes, you do the right thing and use these funds to pay for college expenses.

Student Loans

The absolute last funding option you should consider is going into debt to get a college education. It may be a necessary evil, but it should be used with great caution. Debt should only be used if your degree is going to be in a profession that is in great demand, assuring you of a good-paying postgraduation job. Also, never leave this decision up to your child since they never worry about paying the loan back because that isn't remotely a concern of theirs at this point in their life.

Also, debt should only be used if necessary to pay for tuition and fees and not for lodging or living expenses. It is insanity to borrow money to put your kid in a dorm or sorority house. Also, be extra careful about borrowing money to fund for-profit vocational schools, which are notorious for ripping off students with promises of great careers that seldom work out.

As you can tell by the tone of this text, I am a nonbeliever in borrowing money to fund a resume. That may seem overly harsh, but let's put this in perspective as the student-debt crisis has become one of the largest financial problems facing this country.

According to a recent article in the *Wall Street Journal,* student loan debt has now surpassed credit card debt by more than $3 billion. That means more money is being spent on student loans than on credit cards every year. Many college graduates have student loan payments that exceed their home mortgage payments. In addition, the default rate on student loans is rapidly rising.

There are about fourteen million Americans with student loan debts totaling more than $1 trillion, according to Experian. The Department of Education data also shows that "the average student loan borrower takes longer than ten years to repay their loans." Research finds that "among those who borrowed for their undergraduate education, only half of those students had paid off their federal-student loans twenty years after beginning college. Average borrowers in this group still owed over $10,000 twenty years after beginning college."

Since I am on my soapbox, I want to address the unspoken problem with college education. In a September 30, 2018, article in *Forbes,* Purdue University president Mitch Daniels was quoted as saying, "The only costs that have outrun health care in the last three decades are college tuition, room, and board." Part of the glaring solution to funding a college education is reducing the cost and providing for more state, alumni, and joint partnerships with business and industry. If you lower the cost of education for the student, you directly reduce the savings burden on parents, students, and family members. Mr. Daniels's solution for Purdue was to freeze student costs at 2012 levels.

Daniels also introduced the concept *income-sharing agreements*. Income-sharing agreements allow eligible students to assign 3–5 percent of their future income for an agreed-upon number of years after they graduate. Repayments are capped at somewhere around 2.5 times the initial cost. The beauty of this program is that the financial risk shifts from the student to the college since graduates who don't find work pay nothing. This arrangement forces the college to take a direct interest in your collegiate success. Previously, if you borrowed $10,000 and flunked out of college, it was of little concern to the college. Now, the college has a direct financial interest in your future success.

As I close this college-funding chapter, I will acknowledge that those who save and provide for their children's education often get less financial aid because of their financial success. I often hear complaints about this, but it seems ridiculous that a parent would consider reckless spending as a strategy to fund their child's education—in hopes of getting financial aid because the parents are broke. We all know that children are a lifetime investment in love and money. Enjoy them while you can and just accept the financial responsibility that goes with raising children. It really is worth it.

CHAPTER 22

Comprehensive Insurance Coverage:
The Bedrock of a Financial Plan

Insurance is defined "as a contract between an insurance company and a customer that provides compensation for a specified loss, damage, illness or death in return for the payment of a premium." Insurance is always your first line of defense in any calamity that involves financial loss. Do not take insurance lightly; it is the simplest and most effective protector of your assets.

I have had many clients who have been very successful in their businesses and investment activities, but they have unknowingly put it all at risk because of inadequate insurance coverage. They all have insurance, but for some reason, they often do not spend enough critical time analyzing and understanding their coverages.

Insurance is one of the absolute cornerstones of a solid financial plan. Underinsurance, unnecessary insurance, lack of insurance, and misunderstanding insurance policies are very common issues we all face. The effective use of your insurance dollars is essential to accumulating and protecting your wealth.

A recent personal experience illustrates how easy it is to drop the ball on insurance coverages. I am renting a condominium close to my office in Florida, using it as a second residence. I was recently asked by a colleague if I had renters insurance. I said no because if I lost all the contents in my condo, it would not be a significant financial loss. Let me put it this way, other than my sixty-foot television, I would just give away all my furniture after my lease was up.

As I was explaining this, it jumped out at me that I had missed the primary purpose of renters insurance. I did not need the content coverage, but I absolutely needed liability insurance coverage in case of an accident. For example, I have my football buddies over occasionally, and they are all collectively capable of falling off my balcony at the same time. Going without liability coverage would put many of my personal assets at risk in the event of a judgment from a negligence lawsuit. Needless to say, I called my insurance agent and got as much liability coverage as he was able to get me. I want to also point out that without insurance coverage, I would have to hire my own legal counsel to represent me. If you have insurance, the insurance company will step in with their legal staff and take over the case. That is a huge benefit and relief unto itself.

Since I have led in with homeowners insurance, that is where we will start. I will point out key insurance points that you should thoroughly take up with your insurance agent and providers.

Residential Homeowner Insurance

Almost everyone has homeowners insurance since your mortgage company requires coverage up to the mortgage balance to protect them in case of a casualty loss. The insurance company does not dictate most of the other options you have under the policy. Homeowners insurance is on everyone's mind lately as millions of Americans have been impacted by Hurricanes Harvey, Irma, and Florence and the devastating wildfires in the western part of the United States.

Here are some key points to keep in mind:

- Be sure your insurance will pay for the full cost of rebuilding your home. Building costs are skyrocketing with demand, inflation, and tariffs on steel and lumber. The terminology you are looking for in your policy is "replacement value." If you are insured at market or cash value, you are likely underinsured. It will cost 10 percent to 20 percent more each year in premiums, but that is where you live—and your house is likely the largest financial and emotional asset you possess.

- Be sure to take advantage of all the discounts that are offered by your insurance company. Almost all discounts are beneficial to both the homeowner and the insurance company. These include such things as hurricane windows and doors, roof tie-downs, fire-safety measures, security systems, and the like. These can make a big difference in your premium, and they will cumulatively pay off each year with cheaper premiums.

- Understand that homeowner policies do not include flood, sinkhole (for my Florida friends), or earthquake damage—or water seepage and backups. National Flood Insurance (NFI) can be purchased directly from the NFI or more conveniently through your insurance agent. These all have standard limits of $250,000 per residence and $100,000 for contents. You can and should buy additional coverage from your insurance company beyond these limits. It is also wise to buy flood insurance even if you are not technically in a flood zone. Hurricanes, flash floods, and snowmelt are all causes of floods that are occurring more than ever. The National Flood Insurance Program recently reported that 20 percent of their claims come from areas outside typical flood zones.

- You will have standard deductibles set by your insurance company, but you can elect for higher deductibles if you have the financial strength to cover them and if the premium reductions are significant.

- Your homeowners policy will also provide basic liability coverage of usually $100,000 for accidents that occur on your property. Be sure you opt for a minimum of $300,000 in personal liability coverages—and more than that if it is offered. The modest increase in premium is an insignificant cost for the additional protection you get.

- In addition, it is essential that you purchase an *umbrella liability policy* that will kick in after your homeowner limits are exhausted. These are sold in $1 million increments, and I suggest getting the maximum amount of $5 million. These premiums cost around

$200 per million of coverage and are an absolute bargain for the protection and comfort you get. I just increased my umbrella policy from $2 to $5 million for a modest total annual premium of $855.

- Also, be sure you coordinate with the liability limits on your automobile coverage since your umbrella policy will apply in an automobile accident. Be certain your umbrella policy also covers uninsured motorists because that is the most likely accident you may incur, and this is an area where people are most underinsured.

I am going to say this again. If have any substantial wealth and do not have an umbrella policy, you are a complete fool. There is no nice way to put that.

Keep in mind that your policy will only pay a small amount of around $2,500 for jewelry, collectibles, and similar items. You can pay for additional coverage for these items.

Lastly, you can ease the claim process by taking photos and videos of your furnishings and personal property. We all have smartphones, so be sure to update this every year and have copies on multiple devices so you can document your claim easily in the event of a loss.

Automobile, Boat, and Vehicle Insurance

The most dangerous asset you own—and the one that could cause you the most financial loss—is your car or boat. We have all become less attentive as we drive because of smartphones and interactive communication panels in our vehicles. We all know that a quick lapse can result in a tragic accident, causing severe injury to yourself, your passengers, and other innocent parties.

Possibly more troubling is that according to the Insurance Research Council, in 2017, 13 percent of all drivers had *no* insurance. In Florida, 27 percent of all drivers are uninsured, and several states are in the 20 percent range even though all states require basic auto insurance.

Equally troubling is that a substantial number of drivers are *underinsured*. For example, Florida only requires you to carry $10,000 in personal injury protection (PIP) and $10,000 of property damage liability.

It is beyond obvious that such absurd basic coverage would not begin to cover an accident of any severity.

You cannot control the coverage that other drivers carry, but you can protect yourself and your assets by getting a comprehensive auto policy that addresses these problems.

Let's attack the lack of liability coverage first. Assume your mother-in-law calls while you are driving and lets you know she will be spending the entire holiday season with you. In a moment of distress and confusion, you jump the curb, pop a fire hydrant, and drive through the showroom window of Ripley's Believe It or Not, destroying the wax replica of Abraham Lincoln, their prized possession. You get banged up a bit in the accident, but fortunately, you are well insured with a sound insurance company. After you get yourself under control, you place a call to your insurance company—and they pretty much take control of everything.

Lawsuits fly from several flooded businesses, and Ripley's files a lawsuit for loss of income, property destruction, and the loss of the famous replica of Honest Abe. Your insurance company appoints legal counsel for you, arguing that you were blinded by the reflection off Abe's gold tooth, and you assert that Ripley's purchased Honest Abe from a garage sale in Antigo, Wisconsin, years earlier in exchange for some venison jerky.

Unfortunately, the judge rules for the plaintiffs and issues monetary awards totaling $2.1 million. Good planning and good fortune saved the day as your combined auto and umbrella liability limits were $2.3 million, covering the entire bill, including legal fees. You recover nicely as your mother-in-law nurses you back to health on a diet of buttermilk and raisins.

Life Insurance—Actually It Is Death Insurance

The life insurance industry has a clever way of disguising many of their products with flowery ads of home life and families. The stark reality is that life insurance is not life insurance at all. It is death insurance, and it is an essential part of your financial plan—but only when and if you need it. All mothers and fathers need life insurance in the event of their untimely death, so spouses and children can replace the deceased parents' earnings with the proceeds from a life insurance policy. Most parents are underinsured if they have small children. In January 2017, the Department of Agriculture released a study showing that a child born in 2015 would cost a family $233,610 to raise that child until age eighteen. Stack college costs on top of that, and it is enough to consider just getting a second dog. All kidding aside, if you have children, you likely need a million dollars' worth of *term life insurance*. ValuePenguin recently analyzed multiple insurance companies and noted that on average a thirty-five-year-old nonsmoker could get a million-dollar, twenty-year term life insurance policy for about $1,400 per year.

If you are single, or you are older and your children are grown and gone, you may not have any need for life insurance. Regardless, term insurance is simple and effective and is the only efficient life insurance type you should ever buy. Insurance companies are famous for telling you not to waste your money on term insurance and buy whole life, universal life, variable life, and other so-called cash value policies. These policies combine term insurance with long-term tax-sheltered savings plans. The problem with these policies is that they are designed to be held for life, and there are significant up-front costs and commissions built into these products. That is why they are popular with insurance companies.

You should not combine investments and life insurance into an insurance policy. It just does not make financial sense. Purchase term insurance, take the difference in premium, and invest it regularly as discussed throughout this book. I often see someone who buys a whole life policy based on what they can afford, and their death benefit is way below what they need. In the example above, if that thirty-five-year-old can only afford $1,400 per year and had bought a whole life policy, he or she will only get a death benefit of about $150,000 along with some modest cash buildup.

You should separate your insurance needs from your investment activities. Your life will be simpler—and you will be much better off financially in the long run—if you divert premium dollar differences to a low-expense investment strategy.

I do have one caveat before leaving the life insurance arena. Business arrangements involving life insurance and disability insurance often play an important role in stabilizing a business if a major owner dies or is disabled. Cash-value policies do serve a key role in insuring business owners in buy/sell agreements and other key employee arrangements. Also, stick with large highly rated insurance companies that are name brands and have been around a long time, since your insurance is only as good as the financial health of your insurance company.

Disability Insurance: Insuring Your Largest Asset—Your Paycheck

It may surprise you that, as reported in a 2011 Social Security Administration study, if you are in your twenties, you have a one in four chance of incurring a disability lasting more than three months prior to age sixty-five.

The Hartford reported in a 2011 study that only 49 percent of American workers have short-term disability insurance, and only 44 percent have long-term disability insurance. The possibility of a disability is dramatically more likely than an untimely death. Secondly, a disability with a loss of income is a problem for all workers—whether you are single or not. If your paycheck stops, who will pay your bills? Even if you have significant savings, do you want to exhaust your savings without disability insurance? Not likely—so how do we address this situation with insurance?

Your first line of defense is to sign up for long-term disability with your employer. AARP reported in the summer of 2018 that the average cost of a group policy with an employer is about $40 per month. You should not pass on this. The obvious problem with these policies is that they only cover you as long as you are with your current employer. If you lose or leave your job, you would be without coverage.

The more permanent solution is to purchase private disability insurance that will be with you for as long as you pay the premiums. A general rule of thumb is that a permanent disability policy is going to cost 1–3 percent of your annual salary. There are many factors to consider, and I will address them along with my recommendations, which are based heavily on cost/benefit:

- Insure 60 percent your salary since this benefit is not taxable. This should get you close to your current take-home pay.
- The waiting period is a big factor in pricing. I recommend that you opt for a ninety-day waiting period. Your first step in any financial plan is to have at least ninety days of living expenses saved in readily available cash.

- Be sure the policy defines a disability as not being able to work in your occupation—not in any occupation. The latter means that if you are able to work in any occupation, you would not be covered. That is not a good choice.
- The length of your coverage period is also a big factor in the cost of the policy. I believe a five-year period is reasonable, but you should go longer if you can afford it.
- Be sure the policy is noncancelable, which means your insurance company cannot cancel the policy or raise rates if you change jobs.
- Lastly, your age and health obviously come into play. I cannot help you there other than to say take care of yourself since health pays in many ways, including your financial situation.

So there you have it. Hopefully, you have grasped the important role insurance plays in building and protecting yourself and your assets. Find yourself a competent and diligent insurance professional; they are a very valuable part of your financial team.

CHAPTER 23

Leaving Your Legacy: Generous People Prosper Financially and Spiritually

A *Forbes* article on health care in June 2017 noted that, based on a study by Northwestern Mutual, "Giving back to the world is one of the most therapeutic things we can do for ourselves." The article points out that even MassMutual's recent ad campaign proclaims, "Our happiness is gained through others."

This may sound a bit old-fashioned, but many behavioral studies have shown that generous people are happy people. My professional experience certainly validates this. My clients who are benevolent are my favorite and warmest clients. They are indeed happier and more engaged in life than clients who are focused on getting things and achieving country club and yacht club status. (By the way, I have nothing against either. I like boats and golf.)

I find that one of the most profound questions you can ask anyone is "How do you want to leave your legacy?" If you don't plan for it, your legacy will be determined by others—and that legacy might not be what you think it will be or want it to be.

One might sarcastically respond by saying, "Who cares? I will be dead and gone."

I always challenge that statement by saying, "Your legacy does significantly affect your spouse, your family, your relatives, your friends, your business—or prior business—and the community you live in. You may want to reconsider and work on a legacy of love and respect for you and all the people you touch in life."

But let's back up a bit. I believe you should plan and live your legacy while you are alive and can enjoy and participate in it. Your postdeath legacy will take care of itself nicely if you set the stage while you are alive and well.

I would like to start with a couple of actual experiences that illustrate the power or lack of planning and participating in their own legacy.

The first story is about two successful businesspeople who retired about the same time and knew each other very well. Max was a prominent businessman for many years, and Lawrence was a prestigious attorney who headed up a large law firm for many years. Both were very active and highly visible in the business, social, and charitable communities.

Upon retirement, they were both well-off financially, but neither of them continued their philanthropic ways, and they both discontinued their community service upon retirement. Essentially, their legacies were fleeting and vanished quickly.

I have been told by numerous executives that after retirement, your business legacy diminishes quickly as everyone moves on with their lives, and you may be quickly forgotten unless you continue give back to your community both financially and with your time.

The true story about Max and Lawrence goes like this. I was talking to Max a few years after he retired, and he said he had a funny story to tell me. He went on to say that he literally ran into Lawrence at a Publix supermarket as they pushed their grocery carts past each other.

As they were passing each other, Lawrence said, "Hey, Max, do you remember when we were both big shots just a few years ago? Look at us now—pushing grocery carts at Publix and both pretty much forgotten."

Max said they both got a hearty laugh over it, but the underlying reality was that it was really a sad story and not a funny one. Two men who were everything at one time had slipped out of sight and relevancy because they had failed to establish a lasting legacy. That was a sad and lonely outcome that did not have to end that way!

The next true story is much more uplifting. Wallace and Edna have been friends of mine for more than twenty-five years. Wallace was very successful in the financial-services arena, and Edna had been in the health care industry for many years. They recently retired with lots of investments and large IRAs that they had accumulated over the years from pension rollovers.

When I met with Wallace and Edna, they told me they had been blessed. Their children were financially sound, and Wallace and Edna wanted to start giving back to the community that had made them successful. They were not naïve to some of the tax advantages of charitable giving, which is why they initially sought me out. They simply wanted to maximize their charitable giving while both living and later upon their demise.

After explaining some charitable giving options, they decided to give away at least 50 percent of their total annual income, which was sizeable. They continue to do this to this day, and their trust documents provide that most of their wealth will go to the charities when they pass away. These are two wonderful and happy people who have lived a comfortable life but have found enrichment in helping others. An interesting note is that they usually make gifts anonymously, but they also enjoy the recognition they get from their favorite charities.

The point of this last story is not to suggest that you should give away 50 percent of your income since very few of us will ever have that luxury, but it illustrates the power of giving regardless of the size of the gift. Giving based upon personal ability has proven to make people feel good about themselves—and they typically live happier and more active lives.

Also, do not downplay the gift of your time, which is something we all can give. In fact, many of my wealthy clients tell me it is a lot easier to write a check than it is to volunteer your time. Gifts of money and time are powerful and rewarding to both the giver and the charity.

One of the challenges I have with clients is that most of them are self-made, and they vividly remember how difficult it was to accumulate their wealth. The challenge is to comfort them and convince them that they have more money than they will ever need—and that they may want to enjoy the satisfaction of giving some of their financial blessings back to those who are not as fortunate.

I often point out that their children and grandchildren will duly celebrate your frugality after your demise; they will have no problem flying first-class, buying that Porsche 911, or better yet stop working altogether because it's too much like work.

It is now time to look at the powerful tax tools you can use to have the IRS help maximize your charitable gifts. Using the tax laws to your advantage is both your right and privilege as Congress wrote the laws to encourage gifting to charities.

The Tax and Jobs Act of 2017 has in most cases made charitable giving even more tax friendly. The biggest thing the law did was to eliminate the "phaseout" of your charitable deductions. Prior to 2018, many people lost their charitable deductions because as their taxable income went up, their charitable gifts were phased out. Your charitable gifts are now deductible in full, assuming that you are itemizing your deductions, and not just using the standard deduction. For example, a gift of $1,000 for someone itemizing their deductions who is in the 32 percent tax bracket would only cost them $680 out of pocket because of the tax savings.

The following is my list of tax favored gifting strategies, going from the simplest to the more complex.

Modest taxpayers should consider "bunching" your charitable deductions and property taxes into one year so you itemize one year and take the $24,000 "freebie" standard deduction the next year. Let me give you very simple example. Assume you have $10,000 of mortgage interest, $5,000 in state income taxes, $5,000 in property taxes and $4,000 of charitable gifts. At this point your standard deduction and itemized deductions are exactly the same at $24,000 each, rendering your itemized deductions worthless.

So let's change our tactic and pay your 2018 property taxes in January 2019 and your 2019 property taxes in December 2019. You also delay your 2018 $4,000 charitable deduction by a few days and pay them in January 2019 and then pay your 2019 charitable gifts on December 30, 2019. By bunching these deductions, your tax return now looks like this:

	2018	2019
Standard Deduction	$24,000	$NA
Mortgage Interest	14,000	14,000
State Income Tax	5,000	5,000
Property Taxes	0	10,000
Charities	0	8,000
Total Itemized Deductions	$NA	$37,000

By simply timing your deductions, you save almost $4,000 in federal income taxes at a 30 percent rate ($37,000 − $24,000 = $13,000 x 30 percent = $4,000). This tactic can be used by almost everyone.

For my investor friends, the most beneficial tax trick is to give appreciated stocks directly to your charity to get a "double-whammy" tax deduction. Let me show you how it works. Assume you are itemizing your deductions and have a stock worth $60,000 that you paid $10,000 for years ago. Assuming a capital gain tax rate of 23.8 percent (20 percent + 3.8 percent health care tax), you would pay income taxes of $12,000 on the sale of that appreciated stock.

If you give the stock directly to the charity, you not only avoid the $12,000 capital gain tax—and you also get a $60,000 charitable deduction on top of that. This reduces your taxes by $18,000 in the 30 percent tax bracket. Incredibly, the charity gets the full $60,000, and it only costs you $30,000 because of your double-whammy tax savings ($60,000 − $12,000 − 18,000 = $30,000). You have just doubled your charitable deduction at the gracious expense of the IRS and American government.

Donor-advised charitable funds have exploded in recent years, and the new tax law changes make this one of the most powerful tax-saving tools available to individuals.

A donor-advised fund is a bit like having your own personal charitable savings account. A donor creates an account and makes a contribution of cash, appreciated stocks, restricted stock, real estate, privately held stock, or maybe even art. The incredible benefit of this tax strategy is that you get a full tax deduction when you put the money into the donor-advised fund, but you can decide later as to whom and how much is to go to your charity of choice. Although the gift is irrevocable when given to the donor-advised fund, you still control the funds over a long period of time.

Commercial donor funds such as Fidelity Charitable, Goldman Sachs Charitable Gift Fund, Schwab Charitable, and Vanguard Charitable now have more than $85 billion under management according to a Bloomberg release on October 6, 2018.

Donor-advised funds were actually conceived by community foundations decades ago and remain a popular donor vehicle for local benefactors. The reason for this is that local community foundations have a good understanding of the area's charitable organizations and offer personal philanthropic consulting in your own backyard. Community foundations are just a different variation of the donor-advised fund, but they operate with local control with the same tax benefits.

I personally prefer community foundations to the Wall Street funds because they are managed professionally by a local board of directors, and you are dealing with people who you know, trust, and live with. Either way you go, the tax benefits are very compelling.

Let me now unleash the crazy tax and financial benefits you can achieve with donor-advised funds. I will also compare donor-advised funds to *private foundations*, which were previously my favorite wealthy-person tax strategy. It is now a distant second for the reasons you will see below:

Gifts of Cash

- Donor-Advised Funds. You can contribute up to 60 percent of your adjusted gross income and get a full tax deduction.
- Private Foundations. Your gift is limited to 30 percent of your adjusted gross income.

Publicly Traded Securities and Restricted Stock

- Donor-Advised Fund. Your gift is limited to 30 percent of your adjusted gross income.
- Private Foundation. Your tax deduction is limited to 20 percent of your adjusted gross income.

Closely Held Stock

- Donor-Advised Fund. Your tax deduction is limited to 30 percent of your adjusted gross income based on the objective appraisal of the fair market value of the stock.
- Private Foundation. Your tax deduction is limited to 20 percent of your adjusted gross income based on the cost basis of your stock, which is usually dramatically lower.

Real Estate

- Donor-Advised Fund. Your tax deduction is limited to 30 percent of your adjusted gross income based on the appraised fair market value of the property.
- Private Foundation. Your tax deduction is limited to 20 percent of your adjusted gross income based on your cost basis, which is usually dramatically lower than the fair market value.

Keep in mind that, in both cases, deductions that are limited by adjusted gross income can be carried forward an additional five years and used on future tax returns. This is a huge benefit.

Both strategies give you an immediate tax deduction within the limits described, both reduce estate taxes, both provide for tax-free future growth, both provide control over your investments, and both allow you to "donate and deduct now" and decide later as to whom and when the charity will get the funds. However, keep in mind that private foundations do require you to donate 5 percent of your private foundation assets each year.

Both strategies also allow for successors to manage your funds after your death. You can name your children as successors upon your demise so your legacy can continue for generations.

The private foundation is a living legal entity that goes on in perpetuity. The grantor can establish a board of directors of family members, friends, and professionals. Also, the private foundation can pay a family member or an outsider a reasonable salary or fee to manage the foundation.

I will now illustrate the tax benefits that a friend of mine was able to obtain by using the strategy we just discussed. He was fortunate enough to receive thousands of shares of stock in a public company in exchange for the stock of his closely held corporation. The public company shares became extremely valuable over a short period of time, making my friend very well-off within a few years of the original transaction.

He set up a private foundation at that time. If it was 2019, we likely would have used a donor-advised fund instead. Assume for these purposes that a $2 million gift of public company stock was made to a donor-advised fund in 2019, at a tax rate of 37 percent. The following are the results we would get from making this charitable gift:

Value of gift (now in your personal gift account)	$2,000,000
Avoidance of 23.8 percent capital gain	
Cap Gain ($2,000,000 – 27,000 cost) X 23.8 percent	(470,000)
Charitable Tax Deduction Benefit	
($2,000,000 x 37 percent)	(740,000)
Actual Net Cash Cost	$790,000

So you can see that we merely moved $2 million from one account to another, all under control of the gift maker, while saving $1,210,000 of income taxes. To put it another way, you now have a personal charitable gift account that only cost you $790,000. That is one hell of a good deal and illustrates the power of some of these tax-saving strategies.

You may be saying that this is wonderful for rich people but not so much for the rest of us. That is not entirely true as you can open a donor-advised fund for as little as $5,000. If you bunch your charitable deductions like we discussed above, this strategy can work for almost anyone.

We are going to close this chapter by going back to where we began by saying that "generous people prosper financially and spiritually." To put it another way, "good things happen to good people." Best of all, perhaps on your Judgment Day in the land beyond, you can call in a favor—and it will likely be answered.

CHAPTER 24

Be Careful of Things That Go Bump in the Night: Be Prepared for the Unexpected and the Imminent—Your Entry through the Pearly Gates

---

Getting your personal and financial affairs in order is one of the most important things you will ever do. Unfortunately, since it is not pleasant to dwell on such things, getting your house in order is often left undone or is done carelessly. This is a naturally difficult subject, but it is one we all must deal with.

We will not start with your last will and testament since that is a bit grim, but it is something we will get to later. We are going to start with three documents that everyone should have in place, and they all deal with situations when you are alive.

The first critical document is known as a *living will*. It directs your family, physicians, clergy, lawyer, hospitals, and the courts to allow you to die with dignity. It essentially states that in the event of a confirmed terminal condition that the following are your directives if you are incapable of making decisions:

- You want to be removed from all artificial means and machines that merely sustain your bodily life in a terminal situation.
- You do not fear death and want to be taken off intrusive medical maintenance and be free of hopeless pain.

The document appoints a loved one to make medical treatment decisions on your behalf.

The second key document is the *durable health care power of attorney*. This document is more comprehensive and appoints a loved one to have the authority to make health decision on your behalf "whenever and for so long as you are unable to make or communicate decisions regarding your health care." This document is very explicit in giving your agent virtually total control of your medical situation when you are unable to do so. The key difference from the living will is that the durable health care power of attorney comes into play in nonterminal situations. For example, if you had a severe concussion, your agent could make decisions on your behalf until you are capable of making your own decisions again. This keeps the medical and legal communities out of your life during a difficult time.

The final living document we want to discuss is the *durable power of attorney*. This is an important and powerful document, but it should be used with a bit of caution. The durable power of attorney gives the person you appoint full authority to manage your financial affairs. Be aware that this document is effectively in force as soon as you sign it. It should only be granted to a trusted spouse or loved one because they will have the ability to control your financial assets.

The durable POA is especially useful when someone is incapacitated due to an illness or injury. Obviously, it has to be executed while you are still fully aware of what you are signing. Again, it is a terrific document when someone is incapacitated because of an accident or unexpected illness.

However, as I stated above, it conveys these powers to your agent even when you are perfectly healthy. Granted, your agent must act in your best interest, but it does give your agent substantial power over your assets. Accordingly, you should discuss the potential consequences of a durable power of attorney with your personal attorney.

It is now time to move on to your last will and testament. Unfortunately, in many cases, your will is rendered meaningless—even if drafted by the best law firm in the country. Let me explain why. The following assets do not follow the terms of your will because unless you name your estate or a trust as the beneficiary of these assets.

Life insurance is paid to the beneficiary you name in the policy. Typically, this is a spouse or a child, but it could be an ex-spouse, a wayward child, or a relative you haven't seen in years and can't stand anymore.

I cannot emphasize enough how important it is to review your beneficiaries annually to be sure the person you have named as beneficiary is the person you want your asset to go to.

Most couples and many parents hold bank accounts, investment accounts, and real estate in *joint tenancy*. This is a form of legal ownership that means that when one of the owners die, the other joint tenant (owner) inherits the entire account, no matter what your will says.

Individual retirement account (IRAs) require that you name a beneficiary. If you named your ex-spouse from twenty years ago as beneficiary and did not update your account, your ex-spouse will inherit the account even if your will says your ex-spouse should not get any of your assets under any conditions. Again, be certain you know who your beneficiaries are and review them each year.

Your 401(k) plan account works exactly like your IRA. Your named beneficiary will get your 401(k) account, regardless of what your will says.

Annuities also require that you name a beneficiary, so beware since the beneficiary will get your annuity upon your death despite your will.

Keep in mind that there is nothing wrong with naming beneficiaries as part of your estate plan, but just be aware of the consequences. This works fine in most simple situations, but keep in mind, there are very few simple situations.

If you want all of your assets to follow the directives of your will, you will have to name "your estate" or your "revocable living trust" as the beneficiary. This will then pool all of your assets, and the assets will then follow the terms of your will or trust. As you can see, things are now getting more complicated, but I will work you through some of those complications shortly.

Let's begin with the structure that I believe works for most people. Have a competent attorney who specializes in estate matters draft your documents. Agree to a fee in advance. Think of this as an investment in your future—and not as an attorney fee or an expense.

Remember that if you die without a will (known as dying intestate), your assets will follow your beneficiary designations, as discussed above, with the balance going according to the state law. This state-directed payout likely will not be the way you want your assets to go.

I often hear people say, "It will be somebody else's problem when I die—so who cares?" The reality is that most of us do care who gets our assets, and we do not want to put our families and loved ones through chaos when we die. Why would anyone work a lifetime building wealth and then let a judge determine who is going to get their hard-earned assets? For starters, it is essential that a professional prepares your will and estate documents.

Be very careful as to whom you name as the *executor* of your estate. People often name executors based on family hierarchy, such as the oldest child or a trusted friend or relative. Scratch all of that and look for a person who has the financial and administrative skills needed to settle an estate. This person must be extremely ethical and organized. This often is not a family matter. I have seen many estates in turmoil because a family member is named executor, and siblings are concerned about stealing or the complete incompetence of the sibling/executor.

I recommend that in a reasonably large estate (more than $1 million in assets) that a corporate trustee or a professional fiduciary be named the executor. Although there will be a modest fee involved, it will provide for an honest accounting, a faster settlement, and significantly less family tension. Many banks have trust departments that can handle this for you.

One of the most troublesome things that get overlooked is how you want your personal property to go. This could be jewelry, furniture, collections, art, and anything else that could create family tension after your death. Leaving a signed and notarized list of what and to whom it should go will remove most of this tension and turmoil. Sounds crazy, but there is often great emotional attachment to certain things, and deciding who gets what can avoid perhaps the biggest family fight ever. You may also want to explain how you came to your decisions.

You may also want to put together a separate wish list that tells your loved ones the type of funeral arrangements you desire and your preference for cremation or other special burial instructions. The wish list may include instructions for a funeral dinner, a party, or special travel arrangements for distant loved ones. Actually, the wish list can include just about anything you would like done upon your passing. So be as comprehensive as you would like—and inject a little humor to take the edge off during this somber time.

One of the biggest mistakes I see parents make is splitting their estates equally among their children. This seems like the right thing to do and is the right thing if each child is successful and responsible. The truth is that this rarely happens because children are not created equally. Some children are not financially successful, and others may have been considerably more attentive and helpful in their parents' final years. These are all reasons to make unequal bequests to your children. The important thing is to explain in your will clearly why you decided to make an unequal distribution.

Now that we have gone over the fundamentals of your last will and testament, we must now get into more complex arrangements because life is complicated. These are the common complexities that I often see:

- A fragile marriage that involves children, regardless how long you have been married.
- A second marriage that involves children from different spouses.
- A wayward child who has alcohol or substance-abuse concerns.
- A special needs child or grandchild who will always need help and financial assistance.
- A very successful child who is not in any significant need of any inheritance.
- A wonderful child who is diligent and responsible but is somewhat intellectually challenged. This child works at a steady but modest-paying job. You already help this child and their family financially, and this likely won't change.
- An awful child who has been a nightmare and causes you great discomfort.
- A totally needy child who is always in the middle of some kind of problem and is always asking for money.

Let me try to bring this into focus by giving you a simplified example that will cover many of these situations.

Assume a married couple, Jack and Jill, have had a long and stable marriage and have total assets of $2.2 million and no debt. Assume they have the following children:

- Elizabeth is thirty-five, has a master's degree in software engineering, and made it big with a startup company in Madison, Wisconsin, which makes accident controls for snowmobiles and personal watercraft. She literally made millions of dollars when her company was bought out by Tesla. Elizabeth is married with two small children.

- Albert is thirty-three and is very handy with tools and machinery. He works for a shipbuilding company in Marinette, Wisconsin. He is also married with two children, and he hunts and ice-fishes.

- Mikey, who goes by Mad Dog Mike, is thirty-one and has been a problem since he started smoking and drinking in Little League. He made it through high school and has been in and out of dozens of hospitality jobs from Key West, Florida, to Manitowish Waters, Wisconsin. He only calls his parents when he has a problem, which is often. His parents dread it when his name comes up on the caller ID. They actually have an arrangement that they will take turns taking his calls.

- William, age twenty-nine, is the love of their life. Billy is a sweet child, but he has several physical and mental challenges that require constant attention. He lives at home with his parents and will need financial assistance his entire life.

Jack and Jill have met with their CPA, attorney, and banker and have come up with a plan. When the first spouse dies, the entire estate will go to the surviving spouse. Upon the death of the surviving spouse, the $2.2 million of assets will go as follows:

- Two hundred thousand dollars will go to Elizabeth, and she will also have the power to disclaim this bequest in favor of the remaining children.

- One million dollars will go into a newly formed "Special Needs Trust" for the exclusive benefit of Billy's health, education, and welfare. In the event of the death of Billy, the remaining funds will be transferred to the "Children's Trust," which is described next.

- The balance of the estate of $1 million will go into a newly formed trust for the benefit of Albert and Mikey. BankTrust has been named the corporate trustee, and Brian Fishman, their CPA, was named as executor of the estate.

- The trust provides "sprinkling powers" to the trustee, which allows the trustee to decide how to disburse the funds based solely on the health, education, and welfare needs of Albert and Mikey. The trustee has the right to hire medical professionals to assist in evaluating the needs of the children.

- When Albert turns forty-five, he will be entitled to take 50 percent of what remains in the trust at that time. The remaining trust assets (50 percent) can be distributed to Mikey when he reaches the age of fifty, if he is deemed stable and capable of managing the assets at that time. This determination will be made by the trustee along with medical and legal counsel.

So there you have it—a complicated estate situation that is actually more common than you think. This example is meant to show you the complications life can bring and to illustrate how important it is to get your house in order with the help of competent professionals.

Before we close this chapter, I would like to point out some key things I have observed over the years relative to gifting and bequests to family members.

Large amounts of money given or inherited by children under the age of forty often results in children who are no longer motivated to work—or even motivated to do much other than spend money.

I have seen it over and over again that "instant big money" given to a child who you think is mature may wreck them forever. You add in the spouse, which can really make things interesting as he or she deals with a pile of newfound money. This is the wild card most often overlooked by parents in their planning.

It seems crazy, but my smartest clients are now holding money in trust until their children reach ages forty, forty-five, and fifty. The old model was to hold the assets in trust and give them one-third of their inheritance at ages twenty-five, thirty, and thirty-five. That is too young for most children, and it has been my experience that this is counterproductive and may have a completely unintended result: an unmotivated child with idle time and money on their hands. This is often a formula for disaster or at least problems.

Be extremely careful in thinking through how your inheritance goes to a child who is married. Your child should be clearly advised to keep that inheritance or gift in an account separate from their spouse. Once it is comingled in a joint account, it generally becomes a marital asset, which means that in a divorce, half of your bequest can end up with the divorced spouse.

I have seen on more than one occasion that a disgruntled or unhappy spouse uses a financial inheritance windfall as part of a divorce plan. Essentially, they use this found money as part of their marital exit strategy since there is now plenty of money for the existing spouse to start a new life on their own. Sounds crazy, but it happens. Instead of money making the family unit stronger, it can be the unintended vehicle to tear it apart. Just be cautious and think through all of this carefully with your estate attorney.

Instead of gifting large amounts to a child, I have found the best thing to do is to fully fund an educational plan for a grandchild. The Section 529 tax-free plans are very effective for this. A husband and wife can actually fund up to $150,000 in one year, gift tax-free to a Section 529 Plan for a grandchild. This strategy is a win-win proposition. Making a gift of education to a beloved grandchild will always be remembered by your grandchild, and it will help relieve your child of a huge educational burden.

If you make significant gifts to children during your lifetime, make sure you know what the gift will be used for. I suggest you discuss the gift with your child and have them use it to pay off debt or—better yet—set up an investment account for them.

The use of trusts can almost be a magical instrument in estate planning. A well-thought-out trust can do virtually anything you want it to do, so don't hesitate to use these powerful vehicles. They can be created while you're a live or take effect upon your death (a testamentary trust).

Lastly, if you have a bundle of money late in life, and your children are financially well-off on their own, consider gifting or leaving part of your estate to your favorite charities. The best gift to make out of your estate is to name a charity as the beneficiary of your IRA or 401(k) as all of that money will go to the charity income and estate tax-free. For example, if you leave an IRA of $100,000 to a child, they will pay taxes on it at approximately 30 percent, so they will end up with cash of $70,000. If the IRA goes to a charity the entire $100,000 will go to the charity tax-free. Also, when your time comes, this good deed just might be your ticket into heaven.

Hopefully the tips set out in this chapter will be useful. Estate planning is often put on the back burner until it is too late. It really isn't that difficult if you work with the right professionals. I suggest starting the process today so you can just get it done and over with. Updates will be necessary in the future as situations change, but they will be fairly easy to do.

CHAPTER 25

This Is It—or Is It? When Do I Have Enough to Sail Away?

The ultimate question posed to every financial planner is "When do I have enough money to stop what I am doing and live happily ever after?"

I purposely used the word *stop* instead of *retire* because retirement implies that you are at the end of the road, want to move to a retirement community, play golf, shuffleboard, cribbage, and bingo, and never miss the four-to-six-o'clock happy hour. Actually, that isn't a bad lifestyle for many of us, but some of us just want to change directions and go down a simpler and more relaxed path.

People are now saving and investing much earlier in life so they will have the financial ability to retire or just change their lifestyle to a slower pace and enjoy life a bit more at age fifty-five or sixty. How and what that looks like is completely unique to every situation since every retirement or lifestyle change is truly unique to each individual. I am sure that you understand that each situation is unique, but you still want to know "How much money do I need to do what I want to do—and how soon can I do it?"

The basic formula is really pretty straightforward. You simply take your *total spendable assets* divided by your *net annual burn rate*. Your net annual burn is your annual net income less your annual living expenses. For example, if you have annual net income of $20,000 and your annual living expenses are $70,000, your net annual burn rate is $50,000. In simple terms, if you have $500,000 of spendable assets you would run out of money in ten years. If you have $1 million in spendable assets, you would have twenty years before you run out of money, and so on.

It now becomes very obvious that if you reduce your annual living expenses, your spendable assets will last much longer. In the example above, if you reduced your living expenses to $45,000 a year, your net annual burn rate would only be $25,000 per year. This means if you have $500,000 in spendable assets you would not run out of money for twenty years. If you had $1 million of spendable assets, you would not run out of money for forty years—and just might live happily ever after. These examples are intended to be very simple to illustrate the concept of effectively saving for future retirement or a lifestyle change. We will now move on to a more thorough discussion of how much you need to retire or move on to a more relaxed and laid-back lifestyle.

Let's start by looking at a 2017 Bureau of Labor Survey, which studied more than thirty thousand households and noted that households anchored by a person over age sixty-five spend $49,540 per year on average, compared to $63,450 per year for households anchored by someone under age sixty-five. This data supports my previous premise that life usually gets simpler and less expensive after you retire. Nevertheless, below is the annual average spending by younger and older households according to the study:

Annual Household Spending		
Item	Younger Households	Older Households
Food at Home	$4,540	$3,820
Alcohol and Tobacco	$960	$680
Housing and Utilities	$20,920	$16,670
Clothing	$2,040	$1,190
Transportation	$10,240	$7,510
Health Care	$4,380	$6,620
Entertainment	$3,390	$2,640
Education	$1,850	$390
Contributions to Charity and Other Households	$1,690	$2,430

Contributions to Pensions and Social Security	$7,510	$2,760
Other	$2,290	$2,320
Total Spending	$63,450	$49,540

As luck would have it, this study determined that an average retired household spends about $50,000 per year. This just happens to be very close to the example discussed above, so I will repeat those conclusions to drive the point home:

Burn Rate			
		Average Lifestyle	More Lavish Lifestyle
Annual Net Income from All Sources		$24,540	$24,540
Less: Total Annual Spending (Burn Rate)		(49,540)	(74,540)
Net Annual Burn Rate		$25,000	$50,000
Average Lifestyle Spend Down			
Total Spendable Assets	$500,000	$750,000	$1,000,000
Net Annual Burn Rate	$25,000	$25,000	$25,000
How Long It Will Last	20 years	30 years	40 years
More Lavish Lifestyle Spend Down			
Total Spendable Assets	$500,000	$750,000	$1,000,000
Annual Burn Rate	$50,000	$50,000	$50,000
How Long It Will Last	10 years	15 years	20 years

Now let's move on to an actual case that I worked on recently. It is a more comprehensive and involves a couple who has been financially sound and lives a comfortable lifestyle:

Net Annual Burn Rate	
Wages after All Taxes	$20,000
Interest and Dividends	12,000
Pension and IRA Income	18,000
Social Security	38,000

All Other Income	2,000
Total Income	90,000
Annual Lifestyle Spending or Burn Rate	(130,000)
Net Annual Burn Rate	$40,000

The following is how you calculate your *annual lifestyle burn* or *spending rate*, which is broken down by fixed expenses and controllable expenses:

Annual Lifestyle Burn or Spending Rate	
Fixed Expenses:	
Rent or Mortgage Payment	$-
Utilities	4,800
Property Taxes	6,300
Cable and Interest	1,500
House Insurance	4,600
Car Insurance	4,300
Umbrella Policy	700
Auto or Lease Payment	-
Groceries	15,000
Vehicle Expenses and Gas	8,400
Medical and Dental	13,000
Controllable Expenses:	
Clothes	3,600
Meals Out	15,000
Movies and Entertainment	7,200
Travel and Vacation	24,000
Charities	12,000
Gifts and Holidays	4,800
Vet and Pet Expenses	-
Other Expenses	4,800
Total Annual Lifestyle Burn or Spending Rate	$130,000

This successful couple had more than $2.6 million in spendable assets, so they could live another sixty-five years comfortably assuming that investment returns cancel out the effects of inflation. It was a crazy thing, but this couple was very concerned that they may not have enough money to retire on. It is important to note that as part of their planning they were debt-free and did not have a second home or expensive toys like big boats and the like.

At this point, I thought it would be fun to compare your life savings plan to the purchase of a vehicle. I just happen to own a really fun Ford Raptor truck that gets about fifteen miles per gallon in the sports mode. I also had the pleasure of renting a Toyota Yaris iA this past fall, which got about forty miles to the gallon. So let's say I put twenty gallons of fuel in each vehicle. As you might expect, I could go eight hundred miles with twenty gallons of fuel with the Toyota but only three hundred miles with the Raptor. Basically, I could drive almost three times farther on the same amount of gas if I chose to drive a more efficient vehicle (a much lower burn rate). The moral of the story is that if you have a modest lifestyle, your piggy bank or gas tank will go much further if you reduce your burn rate—or as an alternative, you will need a much bigger piggy bank or gas tank if you go the Raptor route. The choice is truly yours, but you better think about that now while there is still time.

We will end this chapter where we began: "How much money do I need to retire?" Again, on average, retired households spend between $40,000 and $50,000 a year, and they average about $20,000 in Social Security income. That leaves you with a deficit each year of between $20,000 and $30,000 per year, depending on your spending habits. So your choice is to continue to work to close that spending gap, or if you have had the foresight to methodically save over the years, you will have ample assets to retire on your own terms.

If I had to ballpark an investment amount you need to retire at the Social Security age of sixty-six or sixty-seven, I would say you should target at least $750,000 in spendable assets before you retire, and if at all possible, you should target $1.5 million in spendable assets to be comfortable. That may seem daunting, but as pointed out throughout this book, investing early and regularly makes this target achievable. Remember Albert Einstein's famous quote: "Compound interest is the eighth wonder of the world. He who understands it, earns it … he who doesn't … pays it. Compound interest is the most powerful force in the universe." To drive that point home, remember that putting $10,000 a year into your 401(k) plan from age thirty to sixty-seven at 8 percent would leave you with an account balance of $2,030,703 when you retire.

Now that I have given you a target and some encouragement, let me give you a benchmark from a 2016 Federal Reserve Survey on consumer finances. The median net worth of someone at age sixty-five is $1,066,000, and if that household is anchored by a college graduate, the median net worth is $1,511,000.

I am convinced that most of us can meet or exceed those amounts if we just start a modest, disciplined, and methodical savings plan early in life. Living happily ever after financially will be the end result.

CHAPTER 26

How Do I Get to the Promised Land?

I thought it would be fitting to end this book by laying out a simplified framework for how to get there in terms of achieving your financial goals.

Much of this is discussed elsewhere in the book, but I thought it would be helpful to pull it all together for the grand finale. Here is my road map on how to get to your financial goal so you can retire or just change directions earlier in life.

The absolute number one thing you need to do on your quest to financial independence is participate in your employer's 401(k) plan, at least up to the point of getting your employer's matching contribution. This is a no-brainer for everyone—and I mean everyone!

The Bureau of Statistics has reported that, on average, employers match about 4 percent of an employee's contribution to their 401(k) plan. In a simple example, if you are making $100,000 and put $4,000 into your account, your employer would put in $4,000. This is found money, and you just cannot turn it down.

Let's look how this plays out currently and over time. Each year this is what happens:

Cash Flow	
Money You Put In	$4,000
Taxes Saved at 25 Percent Rate	($1,000)
Current Cash Outflow	$3,000

Assets You Own	
Money You Put In	$4,000
Money Your Employer Puts In	$ 4,000 (Free Money)
Total in Your Account	$8,000

The ultimate no-brainer is that your $3,000 investment turns into $8,000 almost immediately. Look at it this way. Imagine if you went to your bank with $3,000 to open a savings account, and your banker said, "Today is your lucky day. If you put $3,000 into our bank, we will open your savings account with a total of $8,000. You will put in $3,000, the IRS will put in $1,000 in saved taxes, and we are going to match the $4,000 for a total of $8,000." How can anyone not do this?

Now let's look at the long-term effect of putting $8,000 a year from age thirty until age sixty when you want to retire or redirect. At age sixty, at an 8 percent average rate of return, you would have $1,059,268 to start off your retirement or your new lifestyle.

These are very modest amounts that almost anyone can handle. Obviously, the more you put in, the more you will have—and the sooner you can retire.

The second most important thing you can do on your quest to financial independence is manage your lifestyle burn rate. Obviously, the less you spend, the more you can save. Here are a few tips to minimize your burn rate without infringing on the quality of your current lifestyle.

Purchase the smallest house you can live in comfortably and buy the least expensive house you can find in a very attractive neighborhood. Remember that your mortgage payment, property taxes, utilities, and insurance move directly with the cost and size of your house. In the simplest terms, if you reduce the cost and size of your house by 20 percent, your mortgage payment, taxes, utilities, and insurance will drop by about 20 percent. Let's now go ahead and quantify this.

By purchasing a smaller house that has a $400,000 twenty-year mortgage at 4 percent instead of a more expensive house with a $500,000 mortgage, it will cost you $29,088 a year compared to $36,360. That's a savings of $7,272 each year on just the mortgage payment. Look below for the total annual savings.

	$500,000 House	$400,000 House	Annual Savings
Mortgage Payment	$36,360	29,088	$7,272
Property Taxes	6,000	4,800	1,200
Utilities	6,600	5,280	1,320
Insurance	3,500	3,100	400
Total	$52,460	$42,268	$10,192

There you have it. By downsizing a bit, you will save $203,840 over twenty years. Invest that $10,192 annual savings at 8 percent for twenty years—and you will end up with $503,718. At that time, you will also become mortgage-debt-free, which will reduce your burn rate by $42,268 per year. This will fit in perfectly with your retirement plan date.

Now that, ladies and gentlemen, is a *perfect financial trifecta*—and you didn't have to go to the racetrack to get it.

Likewise, if you can live with a more modest vehicle or vehicles, the savings cascade very much like the housing example above. If you can drop your car note from $700 a month to $500 a month, that is a $2,400 annual savings. Typically, your insurance, fuel usage, maintenance, and licensing come down as well. Let say that saves you, on average, another $150 per month for a total annual savings of $4,200. Investing that $4,200 annual savings at 8 percent will get you another $332,867 after twenty-five years as you close in on retirement.

Rent, rent, rent, or avoid expensive things like fancy boats, vacation homes, and the like. These high-cost items will stifle your savings plans, and they will drain you and saddle you with unnecessary debt. Studies show that the financial stress of owning things that stretch you financially far outweighs the joy you get from owning these expensive toys and shiny objects.

We have been focusing on your lifestyle burn rate, but the other part of the equation is how much you earn each year. The amount of money you earn obviously affects the amount of money you can save.

So my advice to you is to focus on your profession and find a job that is satisfying and financially rewarding. If you combine a well-paying job with a modest lifestyle, you pretty much have the formula for early retirement.

The final piece to the financial-independence puzzle and early retirement is to invest wisely and methodically over a long period of time. This can be done in tandem with living a very happy and vibrant day-to-day life. There are several chapters in this book that give you various solid and proven methods for investing effectively over time.

Before closing, I want to give you full permission to buy boats, hot cars, vacation homes, and other shiny and expensive things that you have always wanted (as opposed to needed). However, that right and privilege comes with only one condition. That condition is that you have done many of the things suggested in this book, have become financially successful, and have more money than you likely could ever spend.

If you have reached that point, my friends, you have earned it and can do pretty much whatever you would like to do (within reason, of course). As you recall, at the beginning of this book I pointed out that "Money Is Fiction and Does Not Exist until You Spend It," but that right only applies to those who have earned it.

Forge on, my friends, and enjoy life and the journey to the fullest. It has truly been my honor and pleasure to share this book with you. The book is a bit random, a bit rogue, and certainly a bit different, but that is just the way I wanted it to be. Hopefully, you have gotten some tools and tips to get yourself onto the quest for a rich and rewarding life. Again, the pleasure has indeed been mine!